The
JACKASS
WHISPERER

**Check out these other titles
from Scott & Alison**

*UnBranding: 100 Branding Lessons
for the Age of Disruption*

*UnMarketing (2nd Edition): Everything Has
Changed and Nothing Is Different*

UnSelling: The New Customer Experience

*QR Codes Kill Kittens: How to Alienate
Customers, Dishearten Employees, and Drive
Your Business into the Ground*

*The Book of Business Awesome/UnAwesome:
How Engaging Your Customers and Employees
Can Make Your Business Thrive*

SCOTT & ALISON STRATTEN

The

JACKASS
WHISPERER

How to deal with the worst people at work, at home and online— even when the Jackass is you

PAGE TWO
BOOKS

Cataloguing in publication information is
available from Library and Archives Canada.
ISBN 978-1-989025-73-4 (paperback)
ISBN 978-1-989603-11-6 (ebook)

Page Two
www.pagetwo.com

Edited by Amanda Lewis
Cover and interior design by Peter Cocking
Illustrations by Chris Farias, Unicorn Rebellion,
www.theunicornrebellion.com
Printed and bound in Canada by Friesens
Distributed in Canada by Raincoast Books
Distributed in the US and internationally
by Publishers Group West, a division of Ingram

19 20 21 22 23   5 4 3 2 1

www.UnMarketing.com
www.JackassWhisperer.com
#JackassWhisperer

CONTENTS

· · · · · · · · · · ·

WHAT KIND OF
JACKASS ARE YOU?

. . . .

As you read, we encourage you to keep track of your own Jack-assery in the handy-dandy spots provided inside the front cover. For each example, you'll find two possible reactions: the Jackass Reaction (JR) that pays the awfulness forward, and the Whisperer Reaction (WR) that stops the spread. Each Jackass move you've done (be honest here) gets you 1 point. For each Whisperer Reaction, give yourself -1 point. At the end, check out the inside back cover to see how you did. Share your score with the hashtag #JackassWhisperer. No judgement, of course.

ORIGIN STORY

. . . .

It all began back in 2009. Scott was on the train home after giving a keynote speech in Toronto, and checking Twitter (as one did back in '09) when he read this tweet. To protect the identity of the guilty, we'll call him Patient Zero.

> I deserve a cookie. I just watched five minutes of a video of Scott Stratten speaking and didn't shoot myself in the face.

After reading it a few times, Scott replied: "Why the hate?" To which Patient Zero said: "It's not hate, just fact. Deal with it."

Here's the thing: With a platform like Twitter, this interaction didn't just happen, it happened with an audience. A ton of other people chimed in, both in public and private messages, telling Scott not to block or ignore the feedback. "Kill him with kindness," they advised.

No, said Scott. "I'm not the Jackass Whisperer. It's not my job to rehabilitate jerks online."

The Jackass Whisperer message became a rallying cry for everyone tired of keyboard commandos and people who use speakerphones in open-plan offices. It has been quoted with credit (amen and hallelujah), misquoted with credit (seriously, what is a Jackbutt Whisperer?), stolen (ugh), printed on socks and mugs, and even included in Brené Brown's book *Daring Greatly*.

At this rate, it's going on our tombstones: "They died as they lived, surrounded by Jackasses."

So, you're probably asking yourself, what exactly is a Jackass? The original tweet was meant for online trolls and haters, but we realized very quickly it applied to a ton of real-life situations as well. Jackasses are those people who make our lives needlessly harder. They provide unsolicited feedback and begin sentences with phrases like, "Just to be brutally honest here..." They drive slowly in the fast lane and too quickly in the slow lane, reply all, heat up fish in the microwave at work and share way too much information about their cleanse on Facebook. They live in our homes, work in our offices and shop at our stores.

Jackasses are among us, and we have some bad news for you: if you can't spot the Jackass at the (literally any place on the planet), then the Jackass is you.

And sometimes it's us. We realized in writing this book that the person who is constantly complaining about Jackassery may be the Jackass. That was quite the rabbit hole of self-discovery to fall into.

Ten years later, after extensive research, we've come up with a few conclusions. First, there are two sides to just about every Jackass—what someone does (or doesn't do), and our reaction. Jackassery is like a virus—it's contagious. And when we're wronged, we tend to react with equal irritation. Then we take that frustration and pass it along to the next person we meet. Like the new employee at the drive-thru who messes up our order and spills our coffee while apologizing for being in training.

Second, in the face of inevitable Jackasses, preparation is our ally. Is the lineup always super long at the airport? Maybe show up a bit earlier. Is the waiter at your favorite restaurant always rude to you? Complain. Not online, but to the actual human manager, or find a new favorite restaurant. Most of us are irritated by occurrences that are common to us, so pay attention to what gets you ranting and see if you can prevent, or at least ease, the situation.

Third, we are all the Jackass. We've all done these things, and we've had almost all of them done to us and reacted badly. No one started it, no matter how many times that excuse got your little brother out of trouble. Own your treatment of others, own your reaction when meeting a Jackass and own the way you carry the experience forward.

An Important Disclaimer

Look, we know the person who cut you off isn't leading a fascist regime. We know they aren't murderers or racists. We know that in writing this book, we aren't solving world hunger or bringing down the patriarchy. So, before you tweet or post about how petty we are, remember this: if we could all just get along better and stop spreading the Jackassery around, we'd have a whole lot more time and energy to solve the big problems.

Writing this book has been a kind of therapy, and it's taught us an important lesson: we were the Jackass Whisperers after all. So, grab your cape and unitard, because we superheroes have a lot of work to do.

THE
JACKASS IN
THE WILD

A Tale of Two Arugulas

. . . .

It had all the makings of a perfect night: Bob Dylan, third-row seats at the historic Beacon Theatre in New York City, and us.

In rare friendly form, Alison was chatting politely to the couple beside her, as a woman made her way to the seat on Scott's left. We'll call her Arugula, so as not to publicly shame her and because we didn't exactly want to exchange names and keep in touch after the show, as you'll soon see.

Also, because when Scott speaks of her, he makes the same face as when Alison tries to get him to eat Arugula (the green).

Before sitting down, Arugula (the person) threw her coat over the seatback of the person in front of her. When that seat was then taken by another concertgoer, Arugula began to mumble complaints to Scott, about how he was wrinkling her coat and how damn tall he was and why would anyone sit so close to the stage when they're *that* tall and so on. Now, he was probably about five foot nine, and how she expected him not to wrinkle a coat that was on the back of his own seat, we will never understand. She punctuated the grumbles with "can you believe this guy?" looks until she announced she was off to find an employee with a booster seat, without even the slightest regard for the crapalanche of Jackassery she'd be creating behind her. When she returned, she was even angrier because the venue, for adults, in the evening, wasn't providing boosters to adults.

Arugula was a gum chewer and chomped loudly throughout. With her mouth open.

After a few more complaints, she tossed the gum onto the floor and proceeded to whip out a room-temperature cheese string from her purse, a snack for toddlers that smelled so bad we hoped it wouldn't distract Dylan from his performance.

And then she started texting her friend (we can only assume it was Satan) with the keyboard sounds on and the brightness set to "center of the sun." She wrote:

Waiting for the show to start, surrounded by smelly annoying people.

Seriously, Arugula? YOU ARE EATING A ROOM-TEM-PERATURE, IMITATION CHEESE PRODUCT MADE FOR TODDLERS. YOU PUT YOUR JACKET ON SOMEONE ELSE'S SEAT AND THEN COMPLAINED TO A STRANGER. YOU PUT YOUR GUM ON THE FLOOR OF A HISTORIC VENUE AND WE ARE THE SMELLY ONES??

As you can see, Scott was all-caps angry, with Alison oblivious and smiling beside him, patting herself on the back for making small talk with strangers. Clearly the universe was upside down.

The show was amazing. As they walked out of the theater, Scott shared his Arugula encounter with Alison and realized that while her behavior had annoyed him, he was mostly angry over the text. A text he had read on someone else's phone without permission (one of his personal pet peeves).

Yep, Scott was being a Jackass.

We're so quick to point out the ways other people irritate us that sometimes we miss the Jackass in the mirror. Remember, when you're out in the wild and meet a Jackass, sometimes you're part of the problem, which is good news because it means you can also be part of the solution. We aren't saying Arugula (the human) was right—her behavior was truly terrible, and according to Scott she tastes like dirt ... wait, that's the other Arugula.

1. The Jackass is a carnivore

· · · · · · · · · · · · · · · · · · ·

When the waiter arrives, this Jackass loudly announces that they're "not one of those vegans!" and proceeds to order a steak, with bacon on the side. Their social media feed is all barbeques, smokers, memes about vegans and pictures of them in their "meat is murder, tasty, tasty, murder" apron.

JR: You change your life as an act of vengeance and become a raging vegan. Fun fact: this is why Alison became a vegetarian.

WR: You've got no beef with this guy; at least you can get him a Bacon of the Month Club membership for Secret Santa.

2. The Jackass is a vegetarian

. . . .

For the sake of simplicity, and knowing that we'll likely hear about it from the vegans, we'll group all the non-meat-eaters together. Now, we aren't saying that being a vegetarian makes you a Jackass (Alison is one herself), but if you shame or attack others, then you deserve the title.

JR: While wearing your PETA (People for the Eating of Tasty Animals) t-shirt, you pull a pocket hot dog out of your jacket and ask if they want a bite.

WR: You're impressed by how passionate they are about animals and commit to watching one or two of those documentaries they never stop talking about.

3. The Jackass is sorry you were offended

. . . .

We assume they skipped kindergarten or wherever humans learn to say they're sorry. We find this Jackass caught in a mistake and flailing madly to shuffle blame far away from themselves. Without a scapegoat, they may sort of apologize, but add a little (or a ton) of passive aggression. This Jackass can be found backpedaling, blaming others, or worst of all blaming the person they wronged, for everything.

JR: You cut and paste their "apology" into Facebook, publicly shaming the Jackass and their weak apology.

WR: You concede that sometimes you are sensitive to Jackasses. And at least they said they were sorry.

4. The Jackass sees you sweat

. . . .

The Jackass loves to point out others' pimples and sweat. They say entirely unhelpful things like, "Are you going on stage like that?" right before you go on stage. You know who noticed that giant, first-day-back-at-work zit you have on your forehead before anyone else? You did.

JR: You smile and reply, "Well, I can always change my shirt, but you can't fix ugly."

WR: You make a note to remember not to wear that shirt for any more presentations, and also never to share space with that Jackass before going on stage ever again.

5. The Jackass doesn't mention the spinach

· · · · · · · · · · · · · · · · ·

This Jackass notices something fixable and says nothing. Their friend has had spinach in his teeth for an entire job interview, and not one of the ten people he spoke to could be bothered to quietly mention it to him.

JR: When you finally check yourself in a mirror, you swear loudly and call out each and every person who failed to let you know. You plan an elaborate John Wick–style revenge plot, assume control of catering and put together a menu made up of the messiest, most-likely-to-get-stuck-in-their-teeth-and-give-them-bad-breath foods ever assembled.

WR: You know it can be hard to tell people about embarrassing things like spinach teeth and open flies, so you make sure to check yourself before presenting anything. You trademark your own pre-meeting routine, similar to the sign of the cross ("spectacles, testicles, wallet and watch"), that goes "teeth, shirt buttons, fly" before you become the center of attention.

6. The Jackass swipes through your photos

. . . .

When we handed you our phone to look at that photo, there was an understanding that you'd only be looking at that one. Not the last ten photos. For goodness' sake, you Jackass.

JR: You keep the grossest image you can imagine three photos in at all times. That'll teach them.

WR: Hey, if they want to look at the 306 photos of your recent vacation to Des Moines, who are you to stop them?

7. The Jackass is a Wide Walker

. . . .

The reason everyone was scared of the frozen fiends in *Game of Thrones* wasn't because of their eternal invincibility, but because in a group of ten, they walked ten people wide.

Like a sick game of Red Rover without the fun of getting to crash through the line, the Wide Walkers look like they're posing for a *Tombstone* or *Reservoir Dogs* poster, taking up the entire hallway at a leisurely speed. They usually can be spotted in school hallways when you're late for class, airports when your flight is boarding or on the sidewalk next to heavy car traffic to ensure you can't step around them.

JR: Winter is coming. And by winter, we mean you. You do your best impression of [SPOILER] and slay [SPOILER] and then carry on to your destination.

WR: Passing on the left and a polite "pardon me" usually does it. Most people don't realize they've formed the Valyrian steel curtain and can't see out the back of their head and have no idea you're trying to get past. Just breathe, Bran.

8. The Jackass wants you to relax

· · · · · · · · · · · · · · · · ·

Though a favorite way for Scott to torture his younger sister, telling someone to relax rarely has the desired effect. Unless, of course, as it is for Scott, the desired effect is having your sister turn a purplish shade of red and reach new, previously undocumented levels of anger. Aren't siblings the best?

JR: The word "relax" turns you into a rage-filled lava monster from the depths of hell. You repeat whatever you said before the "relax" was applied, but this time it's louder, swearier and at a volume sure to attract a crowd.

WR: You take a deep breath and continue speaking as calmly as possible. Remember that in this world where you are surrounded by Jackasses, you've been called to be better and spread a less terrible message. All you have to do to win the Jackass game is be mediocre, because everyone else sucks. Put that on an inspirational poster, with a picture of an eagle crashing into a mountain.

9. The Jackass wants you to smile

. . . .

Stop doing this, you misogynistic Jackass. That would, in fact, make us smile.

JR: You stare them down with the rage of a thousand customers. Possible replies include, "Maybe you should smile less," or, "I can't; smiling killed my father."

WR: You smile. Not everyone can handle your resting face.

10. The Jackass is just telling it like it is

. . . .

People who say they "tell it like it is" or begin sentences with, "No offense, but..." are Jackasses. We wish they'd just admit that they don't care about the listener's feelings, or consequences. If they want their opinion or emotion to be received at the other end of the conversation, they may want to settle down on that "hard truth" business and try being kind first.

JR: You reply, "I'm just going to call them as I see them and tell you I never want to see you again."

WR: The harsh-truthers of the world really feel they are helping, so you take the feedback, but with a grain of salt. You decide whose opinion has value, and these guys are pretty low on the list. When someone genuinely wants you to succeed, they tell you the truth in a way you can hear.

11. The Jackass always has a better story

. . . .

Listen, Captain One-Upper. A conversation isn't a competition. This Jackass would never tell others to have the "worst day" or the "best ever vacation."

JR: Bring it on, Jackass! You name drop and tell them the story about breaking every bone in your body when skydiving with a chinchilla. Let's see them top that!

WR: You only agree to get together with this one when you're in a listening mood.

12. The Jackass and their old ball and chain

. . . .

They insist on referring to their partner in life as "the old ball and chain," even though clearly they're lucky that anyone would commit to more than a week with them.

JR: Guess that means their wife could use a little attention. You make a note to friend her on Facebook and "meet for a coffee."

WR: You smile and make a point to speak kindly about your partner. How about we treat our partners like our friends and be kind?

13. The Jackass's eyes are on their phone

· · · · · · · · · · · · · · · · ·

This Jackass invited us to get together but keeps their eyes in their lap, even when we're talking to them. We get it, they're busy and important, but they know they were the one who asked us to lunch, right?

JR: You compose a passive-aggressive post for whichever platform they keep looking at about meeting a friend-who-shall-remain-nameless for lunch and how rude they are. Then you wait for them to read the post.

WR: As always, you set a good example and keep your phone holstered when meeting anyone face to face. When you're ignored this way, you interrupt Tommy Texter and suggest rescheduling lunch for a time when he's actually free. If it happens again, you permanently reschedule this meeting for "when hell freezes over at never o'clock."

14. The Jackass must have your undivided attention

. . . .

They are furious anytime someone needs to check their phone in their presence. But some of us have kids who may text us in an emergency. Some of us work remotely, and our phones are allowing us to be with them rather than stuck in a cubicle.

JR: Since they're going to shame you for keeping up with your responsibilities the only way you can, you start bringing physical evidence along whenever you meet. Surely your three kids and a paperwork mountain won't be more distracting than an odd phone glance!

WR: When you sit down, you let your lunch date know you may need to check on a few things while you're lunching, so the expectation is set. If you waited for an entirely free hour, you'd have no friends at all.

15. The Jackass is filming

The Jackass never puts their phone down during a concert. They can watch a video of the Backstreet Boys anytime, so why is their phone between them and the real-life Backstreet Boys? They're blocking our view and they're never, ever going to watch that video. The only video that gets viewed less than a phone-filmed concert is a phone-filmed fireworks display.

JR: Funny and totally made-up story, this is how the photo bomb was created. Some dude was filming something, and an innovative Jackass poked their head in and tadaaa! You make it your mission to turn these never-to-be-watched videos into viral sensations, by putting your head in the frame and shouting a dated phrase like "Wasssuuup?" or "What are thooose?"

WR: Who knows, maybe someone really will want to watch that blurry video. Maybe their date couldn't make it because they're in the hospital or doing important charity work, or maybe this is their kids' favorite band of all time (still a bit of a jerk move not bringing them along, Dad). "Who knows?" is your mantra when encountering a Jackass in the wild. You give them the benefit of the doubt and do your best to enjoy the show.

16. The Jackass won't mute their phone

· · · · · · · · · · · · · · · · ·

This Jackass never turns off their phone. Not during movies. Not during concerts. And certainly not during Scott Stratten keynotes. Unless their ringtone is "Poison" by Bell Biv DeVoe, we don't want to hear it. And if it is, prepare to see some dancing.

JR: You prepare a RuPaul-worthy lip sync to "Poison" and pray that today will be the day you finally get to break it out.

WR: You were the one who decided that movie theaters would play a "turn off your phones" video at the beginning of every movie. Your diligent policy work assures better lives for everyone. When not at a movie, you file a complaint about phones to whoever is in charge and as always set a good example.

17. The Jackass needs their phone to poop

· · · · · · · · · · · · · · · · ·

They rely on their phone for everything. They have apps to tell them when they're thirsty, when they have to poop and even when they should stand up and walk around for five seconds.

JR: Seeing someone using this stuff confirms your belief we're in the end times. You set an alarm on your phone for each day at 3pm to remind you to get angry at whoever is closest to you, and develop the practice into an app called UnTinder.

WR: You thank goodness your body came preinstalled with that stuff.

18. The Jackass wants a medal for presence

· · · · · · · · · · · · · · · · ·

When they do put their phones away, this Jackass makes a huge deal about it. We love that they're spending time in the present, but that should be its own reward. We'd rather not hear about the enormous sacrifice they're making by keeping it in their pocket for an hour. There's no sainthood award for the unplugged.

JR: Every time they mention their phone, rub your fingers together to play the world's tiniest invisible violin until they get the message.

WR: It is nice they've made time to be present. You decide to plan screen-free time more than once a month, then maybe they won't make such a big deal about it.

19. The Jackass doesn't need headphones

· · · · · · · · · · · · · · · · · ·

They may own a pair or two, but this Jackass isn't using their headphones for anyone. They listen to podcasts, movies and music and even make personal phone calls on speaker, entirely out loud.

JR: As soon as you hear someone doing this, you google whatever movie or show they're watching and start yelling spoilers as loudly as possible. "OH MY GOD! IN EPISODE NINE, AT THE RED WEDDING, EVERYONE D—"

WR: If someone plays a loud, inappropriate movie out loud on the subway, and you can't hear it because of your noise-canceling headphones, does it even make a sound?

20. The Jackass is a documentarian

. . . .

It seems to us that the ability to take photos and videos of anyone, anywhere should require some kind of training, license and permission. And yet, here we are. This Jackass thinks we're all just content walking around waiting to be captured.

JR: If they want a movie, you're gonna give them one to remember. What should you go with today? No pants? No shirt? Totally naked cowboy with a guitar over your business? There's just so many to choose from!

WR: Basically, you adopt a "nothing to see here" attitude and go about being your awesome self.

21. The Jackass needs a reply. Now.

. . . .

This Jackass gets upset when not immediately responded to, just because the other person has a phone. Our phones are miraculous, and it's wonderful to have the capability to always be in touch. But sometimes we're driving, or at lunch with a friend, or in the bathroom, so just wait a second and we'll pick you and your brother up at school when we get a chance.

JR: You have a system whereby reply time is relative to the number of messages they send in a row. So when Susan sends you eight text messages, all basically asking you the same thing eight different ways, it takes you eight months to reply.

WR: You reply when you can in a single message (like a sane person) and remind yourself to speak to them about expectations and congeniality.

22. The Jackass can't believe you haven't tried troga!

. . . .

This Jackass can't believe you haven't tried treadmill yoga or ahi tuna or read Michelle Obama's book, like aggressively cannot believe it. "WHAT?!" they say. "YOU HAVEN'T SEEN GAME OF MOTHER FLIPPIN' THRONES??!!" They relish making people feel stupid or out of the loop. A Jackass says, "WHAT?! You haven't tried mountain climbing with gorillas in the Arctic??!!" A friend says, "I had the best time on my honeymoon. I think you'd love the emergency room in Nunavut, they're great with gorilla injuries!"

JR: You make up an entirely false activity and explain how *amazing* it was in such detail that the original Jackass will spend the next two months trying to find it and do it. Shame will keep them from asking you for more information, providing the added benefit of not having to see them for a while.

WR: "No, Jennifer, I haven't tried beach ball parkour. It sounds just great. Please tell me more."

23. The Jackass thinks they're Deadmau5

Here's a tip for DJ Jackass: this wedding is not about you. Easy, Skrillex, you're a glorified Spotify account.

JR: In an act of peaceful protest, you sit cross-legged at the center of the dance floor until the DJ plays a full song from a decade that makes sense to you.

WR: You guess this is what the kids are into these days and try your best to keep up. You have a Spotify account, you're still hip, so you shake what your kids left you with and have fun.

24. The Jackass wants to hear the B side

. . . .

This one is for our DJ friends, which apparently we have. You're working at a graduation or wedding and some Jackass keeps coming up and requesting the most obscure, rhythmless songs imaginable. We're super excited the B side of R.E.M.'s *Automatic for the People* is your jam, but that's never going to happen on our watch.

JR: To be truly savage, you'd have to play these songs and wait for the other partygoers to take out B-Side Dude, but you like your job, so that one's off the table. Instead, you play a two-second sample of their request every so often, just long enough to see the joy on their face rise . . . and then be crushed.

WR: You accept requests from the paying customers, and them alone. Why open up the phone lines if you know the danger?

25. The Jackass was raised in a barn

. . . .

This Jackass chews with their mouth open. They exclaim "ew" to anything on your plate they don't like, while using their fingers to grab at the foods they do, without permission. You want to like them, really you do, but you just can't get past their staggering lack of manners.

JR: When you were young, your mom taught you to take table manners seriously. You smack the Jackass's elbows off the table, hit their knuckles with your spoon when they speak with food in their mouth and tell them to chew quietly or there's no dessert.

WR: While you're not claiming to be Emily Post, you certainly know how to behave at a dinner table. You also know that it's rude to embarrass your friend at a meal, so you stick with trying to set a good example.

26. The Jackass doesn't tip

. . . .

This Jackass has a philosophical objection to tipping because it allows employers to underpay servers and fuels the capitalism-driven industrial complex. We know this because they never shut up about it. They may even be right, and we look forward to their PhD dissertation on the topic—but that has little to do with the single mom of two they just stiffed at dinner. Just tip the woman. Life lesson: treat the people who handle your food well.

JR: Well then, let's see how Jackass likes their meal next time with a little something extra in there. Since your customers never tip, you just keep treating them all like crap.

WR: You hate when people stiff you, so you tip your waiters and the cleaners at the hotel, and especially the young man who schlepped your luggage in a crowded elevator up nineteen floors. You tip in other countries, too, not just your local spots. No one has ever said, "That little bit extra to say thank you was *such* an insult!"

27. The Jackass goes above and beyond, in their own mind

. . . .

We hired a plumber once, who arrived on time and adequately plumbed. We paid him the amount requested, and as he was leaving he asked for an online review. Fair enough, Jack, we'd be happy to. Then, as all was well with the world, he added, "I'm asking for the review because I really went above and beyond today."

We beg your pardon?

First of all, as far as we can tell, he didn't go above and beyond in any single way. He arrived, worked exactly within the expected parameters, was paid and headed out the door. Perfectly satisfactory? Yes. Above and beyond? Nope.

JR: Let's see how he likes his one-star review and when we turn him into a story that we share on the *UnPodcast* and in keynote talks and in books...

WR: Your last three plumbers showed up late, left a mess and didn't fix the problem, so maybe he did go above and beyond. Five stars for him!

THE
JACKASS AT
WORK

The One Where Scott Gets a Raise

. . . .

Back in the early 2000s (flashes Gen X symbol, too small for Boomers to see without their reading glasses), Scott was working at his second job, as a sales trainer for a packaging company. It was a pretty sweet gig. He traveled around North America training people to sell bubble wrap. We aren't talking quick Skype sessions or anything—these were three-day training sessions on how to sell air. And you thought your job was bull . . .

His yearly evaluation was coming up, and he was pretty sure trouble was on its way. He wasn't exactly the definition of a good employee.

Before the evaluation, he called home to let everyone know he'd likely be home early, and possibly unemployed. The time came, and he sat down across from his boss, ready to pack up his desk and thank him for the opportunity, when his boss surprisingly told him the year had gone great and offered him a $5,000 raise.

After the shock of the evaluation, Scott went back to his desk and drafted an email home:

Not only did I not get fired, I got a raise! It's going to be hard to do less this coming year, but I'm going to give it a shot! I work for idiots.

And then he sent the email. To his boss.

A wave of panic came over him as he searched for the "unsend" button of his dreams, wildly pinching the cords coming out of the desktop. He worked literally twice as hard to stop the send as he had the entire last year at work.

His boss walked by Scott's office a few moments later and told him it was probably the funniest email he'd ever seen, and wished him a good weekend.

Yadda, yadda, yadda... Scott started his own business. Entrepreneur, after all, is Latin for "bad employee."

Our workplaces are filled with Jackasses. Some of them slack off, expect to be fired only to get raises, and then email their bosses about being idiots. When you put a lot of humans into one space, Jackasses happen. It's just science. There are loud typers and sniffers, overzealous meeting holders and contributors. There are slackers, those who never make more coffee or add more paper to the printer. Someone in every office mispronounces and misuses words, or uses jargon with such confidence they may as well just walk up to a chalkboard and have at it with their nails. When people share a microwave, things get real. That's work.

28. The Jackass is running the marathon

· · · · · · · · · · · · · · · · · ·

Every other week this Jackass in your office is ~~asking for~~ demanding donations for the marathon they're running or the Girl Guide cookies their child is selling. They've decided it's a wise choice to dip into the pool of people whom they irritate on a regular day and ask them for money on the spot. We love a Thin Mint as much as anyone, but this needs to stop.

JR: In exchange for your donation, you ask them to donate to your Toe Fungus Walk for the Cure. It's just you walking to the pharmacy, but that stuff ain't cheap.

WR: You take the path of least resistance and buy a box of cookies or donate $10. It's easier than the fight or *shudder* actually having to do the run yourself. You suggest putting a policy in place at work that would limit fundraising requests to a table or corkboard in the break room, so there's no cornering in the office or donation-shaming.

29. The Jackass is on speakerphone

· · · · · · · · · · · · · · · · ·

This Jackass loves to listen to music out loud at their desk while singing off key, and loves to use the speakerphone for calls, both business-related and personal.

JR: Your taste in music in high school and sharing a room with your little sister has prepared you for this Jackass. Let's see if they can make those sales calls over Metallica's "Creeping Death."

WR: Noise-canceling headphones aren't just for planes anymore.

30. The Jackass labels others

. . . .

This Jackass is an equal opportunity labeler, whether it's assuming Boomers can't use technology, Gen Xers are lazy or Millennials are entitled. They use terms like "trophy generation" while continuing to walk uphill both ways to each meeting.

JR: OK then, if Carol thinks you're lazy, then that's what she's gonna get. Not like you can help it; you were born in 1976. Part of the Boomer generation? Guess she won't be getting any replies to those ... what do you call them again? Emails? She can complain about you all she wants online. You don't have ChapSnat anyway!

WR: You know that by putting everyone into a box, this Jackass avoids collaboration, making any real connections or learning from their team, so you aren't taking any of this personally. What you are going to do is make sure to mention every tech-savvy thing Bob in accounting ever does, because although he's in his fifties, he is basically an innovation genius.

31. The Jackass calls about an email

· · · · · · · · · · · · · · · · ·

This Jackass is proud to have access to email *and* the telephone and uses both with reckless abandon and no concern for overlap. Their favorite call begins, "Did you see the email I just sent?" and their favorite email is about a phone message they left you ten minutes ago.

JR: Two can play at this game, Jackass. You ignore all forms of communication and fax them each and every one of your replies. If that doesn't work, you try smoke signals.

WR: Your response is a thing of beautiful simplicity—once you notice the pattern, you reply asking which format they prefer, and then stick to it. It's the nicest way to call someone a moron we've ever heard.

32. The Jackass replies all

· · · · · · · · · · · · · · · · · ·

This Jackass takes every group email and turns a simple conversation into a chain of epic, and confusing, proportions.

JR: You reply all every time you see one of these chains form and let them all know as a group to stop replying all.

WR: First of all, you never reply all unless absolutely necessary, hoping some of your common sense virtually rubs off on everyone else. Then you set up a filter that blocks a keyword in the email, so you never have to read anyone's Jackass reply-all insanity again.

33. The Jackass needs custom fonts and backgrounds

. . . .

This Jackass thinks digital communications peaked with My-Space, and they insist on adding custom backgrounds and no fewer than three fonts to every email. Their design style was inspired by a *Xanadu* poster. Enough said.

JR: You reply using either animated gifs or multiple fonts per word. You put in the time to make sure each letter is unique and the email unreadable. Comic Sans and Papyrus never looked so good together!

WR: You set your emails to read in plain text only, avoiding this Jackass entirely.

34. The Jackass has an extra-long signature

. . . .

This Jackass has a signature longer than most of their actual emails. To them we say,

Stop it, Jackasses.

Signed,

Scott and Alison Stratten
Presidents and Co-creators of Content at UnMarketing Inc.
Co-hosts of the *UnPodcast*
Co-authors of 5+1 bestselling books: *UnMarketing, The Book of Business Awesome/UnAwesome, QR Codes Kill Kittens, UnSelling, UnBranding* and *The Jackass Whisperer*
Parents to Aidan, Owen, Jakob, Benjamin and Tessa
Humans to Dallas, Lola, Chelsea and Sugar
Oakvillians, Canadians, People of Earth
On Twitter: @UnMarketing and @UnAlison
On Facebook: www.facebook.com/UnMarketing
On Instagram: @UnMarketing and @AlisonRobin
By phone: 1-800-867-5309
By mail: 221B Baker Street

"Don't feed the trolls, you're not the Jackass Whisperer."
SCOTT STRATTEN

"Don't hit your brother, or I'm turning this car around."
ALISON STRATTEN

CONFIDENTIALITY NOTICE: The contents of this email message and any attachments are intended solely for the addressee(s) and may contain confidential and/or privileged information and may be legally protected from disclosure. This message is intended to be read by the recipient. If you received this message in error, please disregard, delete, destroy your phone and bleach your eyes.

JR: You slightly change their legal disclaimer to mention something about the person themselves and see how long it takes them to notice. "This email is written for its intended recipients, and Brad needs to stop wearing hipster skinny jeans and turtlenecks..."

WR: You read and reply like any other email; it's not like you paid extra per line to read it. You know signatures and disclaimers like this are usually mandatory; besides, no one actually reads them.

35. The Jackass can't get enough meetings

. . . .

This Jackass calls a meeting to discuss meeting etiquette. They just can't get enough.

JR: You request to add to the agenda for every meeting a discussion about how there are too many meetings in your workplace.

WR: You show up on time, if not early, for meetings, with bonus Whisperer points if you're early enough to get first choice of donuts.

36. The Jackass is constantly stopping by to distract you

. . . .

This Jackass is especially active in open-plan offices, although they've been known to frequent a cubicle or two. They stop by to discuss the email they just sent you, the meeting they just called for after lunch, the project you're unfortunately working on together, and sometimes just to say hi and let you know they have a case of the Mondays.

JR: You develop an early detection system made up of Ethernet tripwires and MacGyver-like spy cams to warn you of their approach, slow them down, trip them up and generally make your workspace the least friendly place in the office. Also, sometimes you work without pants on.

WR: When the distraction can't be avoided, you smile and give in to the visits. I mean, hey, at least you aren't in a meeting. You've also perfected faking an important phone call just as you hear them approach, and with the magical mime of a wave and a "Sorry, I'm on the phone," they move onto the next victim.

37. The Jackass leaves early and shows up late

. . . .

Cooperation be damned, this Jackass is always at least ten minutes late and leaves at least ten minutes early. They seem totally unprepared for the daily traffic everyone else managed to get through on time.

JR: You call a meeting to discuss "new" technologies such as GPS and Google Maps and include a copy of Captain Late-to-Work's route from home for everyone to evaluate.

WR: You let them know privately that this is affecting everyone because they're such an important part of the team.

38. The Jackass comes early and stays late

· · · · · · · · · · · · · · · · · ·

They practically live at the office, while magically remaining one of its least productive employees. They arrive early, stay late and loudly critique anyone leaving on time with a comment like, "I didn't know we had banker's hours, Jim!"

JR: You leave your car in the office parking lot overnight and take a cab home. When Chad notices, he'll spend all day trying to find you and end up sleeping at his desk. If you're going to be judged, you may as well have a little fun.

WR: You let your work speak for itself and suggest a workshop to help coworkers relate to the out-of-office demands we all have, creating a more supportive and inclusive workplace in the process.

39. The Jackass is always sick on Mondays

. . . .

This Jackass has actually come down with a case of the Mondays, a little too conveniently taking sick days to extend their weekends and long weekends. So frequently, in fact, that you've come to expect the call. Their absence puts an unfair burden on those they work with, work for and manage.

JR: You choreograph an office-wide discussion about just how epic Monday was at work, to be performed each and every Tuesday. Include comments about bonus checks, free donuts and pajama day attire.

WR: If this is your employee, you give it to them straight and privately let them know the pattern has been noted and won't be acceptable going forward. Mondays come each and every week, and you'll expect to see them bright and early, ready to work. If this is your coworker or manager, you file a complaint and let their manager speak to them. It's not your job to babysit them, but it isn't your job to take up their slack either.

40. The Jackass shows up to work sick

. . . .

Even though this Jackass has the flu, they've decided to martyr themselves (and apparently you as well) and show up to work weak, red faced and sneezing. They think it makes them look dedicated, but it actually makes them look like a selfish Jackass.

JR: There are a few ways you could go here, depending on the strength of your immune system. You could approach the martyr, doing your best impression of the close talker from *Seinfeld*, wait for the apex of their sneeze and, as their mouth opens wide, cough right into it. Then run away apologizing for the tuberculosis they now have to be vaccinated against. Another option is wearing a hazmat suit like Dustin Hoffman in *Outbreak* or Brad Pitt in *World War Z*.

WR: You'd rather deal with the sick martyr than Joe in accounting who gets the "flu" every long weekend. You keep your distance, wash your hands frequently and eat your vegetables.

41. The Jackass needs a vacay

. . . .

Trust us, this Jackass has the time to say the whole word. They likely also are fond of saying "yolo" and "fomo."

JR: You start using the word "staycay" to describe your evenings after work.

WR: While you would never use such a word, you too enjoy a vacation and make small talk accordingly. Hey, no one is perfect, right?

42. The Jackass leverages to sell

. . . .

This entrepreneurial Jackass read a book that told them to leverage every opportunity to sell, and they've taken the advice to point. To them, Remembrance Day, Veterans Day and even a personal loss to a coworker or friend are all just chances to sell you their crap. Heard someone's dad passed away? This is the perfect opportunity to market their home organization services!

JR: Shame, shame, shame! We're guilty of this one; some would say we've even built a brand around calling out Jackasses like these, and we stand by each and every time we've done it. A tragedy is the time to help, not market your business. You take the brochure they left in the break room and pin it up on the bulletin board with "What not to do!" written across it in red Sharpie.

WR: You keep your reactions to sleazy marketing ploys that leverage inappropriate holidays and news stories quiet, while quickly unfollowing and/or blocking anyone who uses this type of tactic online and in real life. No more eating lunch with Jeff for you.

43. The Jackass doesn't eat well with others

· · · · · · · · · · · · · · · ·

This Jackass never learned to share a kitchen. They steal your food from the fridge, heat up stinky food in the microwave and leave the coffee pot empty.

JR: You google "worst combination of flavors" and create a banana, mayonnaise and cilantro sandwich, put your name on it and wait for the payoff.

WR: Three words: desk mini fridge. You knew this would happen when you took the job, and you've prepared for the worst. No one is getting your sandwich!

44. The Jackass speaks in jargon

· · · · · · · · · · · · · · · · ·

We need a buzzword dictionary to understand this Jackass. They're really into the synergy of the UX (user experience) and the buying patterns of "Xennials."

JR: You put in the time and learn Victorian-era style English and only speaketh to those folk liketh this, from anon on.

WR: You just roll with it, while secretly playing a game of jargon bingo (seriously—google it; there are boards).

THE
JACKASS AT
THE GYM

An Ode to Swol

. . . .

Our basement could be rented out as a personal gym, with equipment that includes a Peloton bike, a treadmill, a variety of weights and straps, a punching bag and boxing gloves, some kind of climbing apparatus and of course a Ping-Pong table, for cardio. But even so, every week Alison ventures out to the gym or yoga or Pilates class—the exception being between January 1 and the end of February when, in an attempt at resolution avoidance (and, therefore, Jackass avoidance), she stays home.

Years ago, Scott signed up for a gym membership that included a few sessions with a personal trainer who was so incredibly bored that he spent their entire first meeting reading the phone book on his desk. If you don't find your new clients more interesting than the Yellow Pages (at least we found someone who reads that thing...), you should be in another line of work. Business would be so much easier without all these pesky clients, amirite?!

Gyms are Jackass breeding grounds. Take all the factors that make work and school a joy, such as a bunch of humans close together, and add in some fun things like sweat, exertion and competing body image ideals.

Everyone has words that make them cringe. "Bro," maybe, or "moist." Alison's brain shuts down every time someone uses the word "hack." Maybe yours is "Jackass" (although if so, we'd love to talk to you about your book choices). On the *UnPodcast*, we have an entire segment dedicated to made-up words we despise, like "brogurt," for example (yep, yogurt for bros). Here's the thing: for every one of us that hates a word, there's a hundred people who can't say it enough. Since we're headed to the gym, let's consider the word "swol." The *Oxford English Dictionary*, we pray, will never define it, but if you're one of the lucky ones who doesn't know what it means, "swol" means bulked up with lots of muscles. (*See:* ripped. Usually referring to a gym dude with giant, or swollen, muscles.)

We hate the word "swol" and seriously judge anyone who uses it. But here you are, reading this, enraged! You *love* that word. It changed your life! You named your first child Swol. Swol saved your father from a terrible food truck incident in '89.

This section is dedicated to the Jackass at the gym. We shall call him Swol. And he's, ya know, swol.

45. The Jackass hogs the equipment

. . . .

There are two treadmills in this gym, ma'am. If you're using one, cool, we can wait. But if you're sitting there checking Instagram while three people clearly wait, you're a Jackass.

JR: You grab the Big Mac you've stashed in your gym bag and slowly eat it, a foot away from the treadmill.

WR: You grab a yoga mat and work on that core! After that gym bag Big Mac you ate on the way over, you need to do some crunches anyway.

46. The Jackass sweats and forgets

· · · · · · · · · · · · · · · · ·

No one wants to sit on your just-used, all-sweaty bike seat, Swol. No one. Ever. This Jackass knows how to use the equipment; they just don't know how to share the equipment.

JR: You determine what machine is next on Swol's circuit and sweat on it while making eye contact with Swol to assert your dominance.

WR: You're gonna sweat on it anyway, plus now you can use the antibacterial wipes you bought yourself for Christmas!

47. The Jackass is a heavy breather

. . . .

Breathing is a big part of exercise—nay, life. But this Jackass is heaving like a woman who's nine centimeters dilated. They may want to take it down a notch. Their Zen is killing our Namaste. Or whatever hippies say.

JR: You see their loud breathing and raise them loud panting and grunting. Think "Dueling Banjos," a bro version of *Deliverance*, minus the pig squeals and prevailing sadness.

WR: You switch to the Monday evening class where they play music, which really drowns out the heavy breathers. At the gym, you work out to your Beyoncé mix with headphones, and no one's breathing is getting between you and "Single Ladies."

48. The Jackass cancels at the last minute

. . . .

Back in January, during a resolution-filled haze, this Jackass signed up for the 5pm Zumba class at your gym. As the months have passed, they've shown up less and less, but because they never let the gym know, that precious spot sits open and unfillable. They've even managed to annoy the instructor, who also teaches yoga and meditation, so if *they're* angry, you know you have the right to be.

JR: When the Jackass does show up for class, you encourage the instructor to up the exercise level to the point of unbearable. Let's see how this Jackass feels tomorrow!

WR: You let the gym administrator know you want that spot when it opens up at the end of the series and personally promise the instructor to use the spot or let them know in a reasonable amount of time if you can't be there.

49. The Jackass shows up late, expecting a spot

. . . .

They won't commit to a time or place, but prefer to show up when it suits them and expect the class instructor to just make room. After all, the exercise world does revolve around their sedentary and demanding Jackass selves.

JR: Not only are you not moving over to make room, you're going to work out so exuberantly beside them that they'll never come back. Let's see how their tree pose is when you're kicking them in the shins.

WR: Sure, you paid in advance and arranged your schedule to be here, but not everyone has the privilege to do that. The more, the sweatier!

50. The Jackass needs you to know they're sweating

· · · · · · · · · · · · · · · · · ·

This Jackass is oversharing on social media about their workouts. If we hear one more story about their planking challenge, we're gonna find a plank and make them walk off it.

JR: You make it your job to comment on every post about how much you hate their workout and the elliptical it rode in on. Or maybe you'll be extra witty and, for every mile they run, share how many donuts you ate for breakfast.

WR: You're irritated, we get it. These active folks make us couch potatoes feel lazy and inadequate (someone pass the guacamole...). Rather than hate on the fit, you go offline and get some exercise of your own. Or maybe you smile and remember that without active people who share workouts online, most of your beloved fail videos wouldn't exist. You can't delight at someone falling dramatically off a treadmill if there are no treadmill posts.

51. The Jackass shames others at the gym

. . . .

The Jackass takes photos of others on equipment and in the change room and shares them, with mean comments. Do not under any circumstances do this. Most of the time there are two sides to every Jackass, but this is the exception. There's no reason ever to shame someone else at the gym. They're there for themselves, so leave them alone.

JR: You take a picture of the person taking the shaming photos and shame them. The classic shaming of the shamed. Shame on them. Shame (*Game of Thrones* style).

WR: You see this happening and report them to the gym. Immediately.

52. The Jackass calls everyone Bro

. . . .

We're putting this here due to the strong correlation we've found between gym Jackasses and bro Jackasses. Why learn anyone's name, when you can call them all Bro?

JR: You reply, telling them it's pronounced "Bra." And if they say "Bra," you correct them, telling them it's pronounced "Bro." Sometimes you correct them and ask to be called Christinith.

WR: You can barely remember what you ate for breakfast, and you certainly can't keep up with everyone's name at the gym. You'd rather not be called Bro, but at least they said "excuse me" before picking up the weights beside you.

53. The Jackass is very excited about Whole30

· · · · · · · · · · · · · · · · ·

The Jackass is constantly posting about weight-loss tips and food restrictions, usually fad diets they yo-yo in and out of. Everyone needs to know about their bacon-only diet, including their boss, future coworkers, mom, kids, kids' friends and that guy on Tinder they're hoping to date.

JR: You comment on every post, calling their diet insane and unhealthy, upping your shares of anything restricted to them and tagging them accordingly.

WR: You may have an opinion, but you don't actually comment on people's diet posts telling them their bacon diet is insane and unhealthy. Unless they ask for feedback, they don't care about your opinion of their food journey. (Note to selves: add "food journey" to list of most hated terms.)

THE JACKASS AT THE MALL

Thanks a Lot, Carol

. . . .

Alison has what one might call a very task-specific resting face: Alison Mall Face. She would be scoring the lion's share of her Jackass Reaction points at the mall; however, as one of our authors, she created a system by which her Jackass Reactions (she regularly does each and every one) don't get points. The magic of being in charge.

Her shopping dream is "competent disinterest"™—a Jackass-free world where semi-attentive salespeople know their stuff but stop shy of fake friendship and phony compliments. She doesn't want to be called "love" or touched or wildly complimented on every outfit she tries on.

Many years ago, on one of their first shopping trips together in Las Vegas, Alison ignored an overzealous salesperson so completely that Scott followed behind her shocked and apologizing. Who was this stone-faced ignorer of compliments, and should he take her to see an audiologist Monday morning?

He quickly learned that, like her remarkably harsh aversion to the sound of folding and ripping paper, Alison Mall Face was just part of the package. It was actually a pretty common sight, followed closely by her "Alison at a Restaurant with a Close-Talking Waiter" Face.

Over the years, Scott has done a number of undercover shopper trips. His "Are you the sound guy?" look makes him ideal for checking out how stores really treat their day-to-day customers. He once spent an afternoon at the mall being completely ignored before finding Lush, where he was treated to a sultan's tour and came home with $300 in soap. He also once famously recorded himself walking around Walmart to test the Walton Ten-Foot Rule (any Walmart associate who comes within ten feet of a customer is to make eye contact, smile, and ask if they need help), set to "Hello" by Lionel Richie. Spoiler alert: No one greets him at all, or makes eye contact, for the entire video. It's breathtakingly terrible.

Whether it's at the grocery store, a shopping mall or just the corner store, being a consumer is rife with Jackass possibility. Front-line workers are often the lowest paid, least appreciated members of a company's team, while at the same time being the closest connection customers have to a brand. That's a bad combination. When Carol in accounting decided the company should have a no-returns policy, it's the kid at the cash register who's left to handle the angry customers. Thanks a lot, Carol.

54. The Jackass thinks you *need* those jeans

- - - - - - - - - - - - - - - -

It's possible that Alison is the only person in the world hating on this, but she's one of the authors, so this Jackass is making it into the book! This overzealous salesperson jumps on you as soon as you enter a store and tells you that you simply *must* have that item or look *so* amazing in whatever you try on. They call customers "love" and make physical contact whenever possible. Easy, cowboy, take it down a few notches.

JR: As always, you think to yourself WWAD (What would Alison do?) and ignore the salesperson to the point of rudeness.

WR: You ignore what Alison would have you do and invoke your inner Scott. You politely let the salesperson know that you're just looking and that your wife isn't rude, she's deaf.

55. The Jackass sneers when you don't donate at the register

. . . .

We know the checkout person didn't make the corporate decision to ask for donations at the register, but that doesn't mean they can sneer at us if we decline. We're just trying to buy a Diet Coke, Steven.

JR: WWAD? She'd say no to every donation at the register on principle. She eats judgmental looks from front-line workers for breakfast.

WR: You follow Scott's lead and donate whenever asked. What's five more dollars when you're buying two hundred dollars in groceries?

56. The Jackass shows up at five minutes to closing

. . . .

The bane of every front-line salesperson, this Jackass shows up five minutes before close and must be served.

JR: As long as the store is officially open, you're shopping, browsing, trying things on and asking as many questions as possible. In fact, you've brought a list of questions that you slowly take out and recite at a snail's pace to anyone unfortunate enough to be working until close.

WR: You plan all your shopping to be done fifteen minutes to close. You've worked retail, and you've never forgotten to treat front-line workers the way you wish you'd been treated.

57. The Jackass closes at 5:55

. . . .

Alison dated a guy in high school (who she assumes doesn't read our books) who was fired from a job as a "sandwich artist" for closing five minutes early when a tour bus pulled up in front of the restaurant. This Jackass sees closing time as the moment they plan on walking out the door, and customers be damned, the till will be offline by quarter to.

JR: You make it your mission to show up ten minutes before closing, just in time to mess with this Jackass's plans. Every. Single. Day.

WR: You make a note to file a formal complaint with the manager next time you're in the mall. Nothing to be gained from making a kid at the mall miserable every day.

58. The Jackass can't count to twelve

. . . .

This Jackass apparently never learned to count, because they're in line at the "12 items or less" cash register with at least three dozen items. Those lines were created to help move shopping traffic along, but this Jackass doesn't care. There's a reason rules exist. And yes, Pumpkin, they apply to you.

JR: You count the Jackass behind you's items and move the divider to just past the twelfth one, then thank them for picking out all the other items for you. So thoughtful!

WR: You know what you love? Self-checkout lines! The best.

59. The Jackass doesn't care where the carts go

· · · · · · · · · · · · · · · · ·

Like our "12 items or less" Jackass, this person just wants to watch the world burn. They probably don't return their rental cars or put their garbage out properly either. They just leave their cart beside a car and let the universe return it.

JR: You grab as many photos of the culprit leaving their cart as possible, have them designed into wanted posters and leave copies all over the grocery store. Shame is your anti-Jackass weapon of choice.

WR: You take back their cart, as you were going that way anyway. You're sure they're having a terrible morning and are in a rush, so why not help out a little whenever you can?

THE
JACKASS
ONLINE

Pet Parents are People, Too

. . . .

Back in 2013, Alison wrote a blog post about pet parents (for you Millennials, a blog was once a "game changer" that would end all books, newspapers and non-bloggy communications).

The post was the most popular she'd ever written to that point. She hit "publish" before boarding a flight from Toronto to Vancouver with three of our children. By the time they had landed four and a half hours later (Canada is big, people. So no, we can't meet you for a drink because you're visiting Canada. Vancouver is as far away from Toronto as London is), the post had gone crazy and there were hundreds of comments. Most of them furious at Alison.

In the post, she described a conversation overheard in line at a Starbucks in Las Vegas. A fellow drink-awaiter was complaining to her friend about all the trouble it took to get away because she had to find someone to care for... her dog. As a parent of three humans and owner of two dogs at the time, Alison thought this was ridiculous. A dog is not a child, and the care that goes into one is not even close to the same thing.

The post/rant went crazy, and the comments were off the charts.

"Alison shouldn't even be allowed to own a goldfish if she thinks pets' lives' aren't valuable."

"Alison should have her pets taken away from her immediately."

"Some people can't have children, Alison. Does this make their lives less important?"

Jeez, people. All she said was that there is a fundamental difference between a child and a pet. Like how we accept that a pet may need to be put down one day, or how a pet is left in a crate when we go to work or the grocery store; that behavior is kind of frowned upon with children. We never even mentioned, or judged, one's ability to become a parent. But if the house is on fire, you save the children first, right? We aren't donating kidneys to save our Schnauzers . . .

Alison was pretty torn up about the comments. Who did these Jackasses think they were talking to anyway?

But here's the thing. A few years of distance has taught us that when you put your opinion online, no matter how strongly you hold that ideal, you invite the world in. And in they come. Although Alison never said anything aloud in Starbucks that day, she did decide to share her Jackass opinion with the world. And for everyone who agreed with us, we need to be prepared for the avalanche of poodles in BabyBjörns who won't.

60. The Jackass has ten easy steps

. . . .

We're going to save you a lot of money here, so listen closely: the Ten Easy Steps Jackass isn't in it for you. There are no ten (or one, or three, or any number) easy steps to anything, and if one of the steps is buying whatever this Jackass is selling, run, run away. We dream of the day someone can make money selling "The 831 Challenging Steps to Contentment." It reminds us of the old saying, if you want to be successful in real estate, sell a course in how to be successful in real estate.

JR: Whenever you see a post like this, you reply asking why, if they're so successful, are they selling the secret? If it was really so easy, they'd be sitting on a beach, sipping a cold drink and watching the money roll in.

WR: You see right through these listicles to success, take the good ideas and leave the rest. You're also a poet and don't know it.

61. The privileged Jackass

. . . .

This Jackass advises others that the secret to happiness is simply to throw away anything (or anyone) that doesn't bring them happiness. Privilege drips off statements like that. Most of us can't take a spa weekend with the girls to manage the stress of parenthood and/or general adulting. Most of us don't have the time for "me time" or to get to the gym four days a week. What we need to throw away are unrealistic expectations and judgement; now that would make life happier.

JR: Since you're always looking for an easy way to do anything, you're all over these. When you complete each and every step and have accomplished little, you become all-caps enraged. I SLEPT THREE HOURS A NIGHT, DROPPED OUT OF UNIVERSITY AND WORE FLIP-FLOPS TO ALL MY SALES MEETINGS, AND STILL I AM NOT A FORTUNE 500 CEO! RAGE!!!

WR: You appreciate the advice and certainly look forward to a little "me time" as soon as your business has some legs under it and your three kids are out of diapers. You won't be throwing out your belongings, but you will add as much joy as you can to your everyday.

62. The authentic Jackass

This Jackass read a book in 2010 (possibly written by us) and took the whole "authentic self online" thing a little too far. When they offend, they use authenticity as an excuse and advise authenticity to everyone they come into contact with. Their phrases of choice are, "I just call 'em as I see 'em" and "I'm a straight shooter." No, you're not, Kevin. You're a Jackass.

JR: You call it like you see it with Kevin and scan all his posts for mistakes you can leverage. He doesn't look like his profile picture? Bring it up often. Made a spelling mistake? Share that non-stop. When he eventually freaks out, reply, "Haters gonna hate."

WR: You realize that one of the benefits of success is being able to be your authentic self, and you look forward to the day you're successful enough to wear flip-flops and swear like a trucker too.

63. The deep-googling Jackass (a.k.a. Captain Creepy)

. . . .

Meet this person once, online or off, and they rush to their phones to find out everything they can about you. Stat. They follow the rabbit hole back through photos from 2005, liking random ones along the way, and weird you out over coffee as they quote your research papers from college and name places you worked back in the '90s.

JR: You use the internet Wayback Machine (archive.org) to dig up this Jackass's old MySpace or Friendster profile and ask them if they're still the biggest Fall Out Boy fan. Ever.

WR: You note the creepiness and cancel any future plans with this deep googler, but realize this is part of meeting people these days.

64. The Jackass has no shame

. . . .

These are the TMI (too much information) Jackasses of our age. Now that they can share every moment of their lives, they jump in with two feet, warts and all. Literally: photos of both feet, with the warts... This is going to be a shock, but the world doesn't want to hear about your cleanse, see you naked or hear any other personal information more suitable for the doctor's office than social media.

JR: Literally go toe to toe with them. For every picture they share, post one in return. Bonus points for sharing ones that couldn't possibly be yours: baby feet, horse's hoof, etc.

WR: The mute button is a Whisperer's greatest weapon on social media, the online version of noise-canceling head-phones. You won't see their posts but still stay connected, avoiding awkward unfollow conversations.

65. The other TMI Jackass

. . . .

This Jackass may not be sharing their actual warts, but their emotional ones are on display. They share negative personal information to shame others. Even when they don't name the person, it's not hard to connect the dots. We all know that the "idiot husband who didn't do the dishes" is Donald. Venting like this always comes back to you.

JR: You comment on every ranty post, starting with, "Just to play devil's advocate..." and then adamantly defend whatever Donald is up to. "Just to play devil's advocate, a dirty kitchen is a sign of a happy home." "Just to play devil's advocate, kids should really be responsible for their own laundry."

WR: You always set a good example of how to treat others online, so this kind of thing really irritates you. That mute button is going to do wonders for Donald's wife.

66. The Jackass is vaguebooking

. . . .

Have you ever called someone to tell them you'd be calling back later with some big news? Ever dropped by your friend's place to let them know you'd be back tomorrow for an actual visit? Back in college, did you ever tell your boyfriend or girlfriend that you needed to speak to them later about something really important, and then leave? (We know most of you have done this one. You're monsters.) This Jackass has the biggest news to share; they just can't tell you yet.

JR: Fill the comment section with guesses, the more embarrassing the better. Include phrases like, "Have the charges been dropped?" and "Did that rash finally clear up?"

WR: You're excited to hear all about it. Later.

67. The Jackass is a thief

. . . .

The sincerest form of Jackassery, these folks take other people's content and claim it as their own. They consider the internet public domain and scrounge Reddit for clever memes, later posting them without credit. If they copy someone unintentionally and are called on it, they backpedal, call it flattery and continue on their way.

JR: Comment each time and include credit to the original. "I saw that on Reddit too! Isn't r/Stratola hysterical?!"

WR: You keep on scrolling past this wannabe. They lost your trust long ago, so you already never give them your attention.

68. The Jackass is #blessed

. . . .

This Jackass is all about the humblebrag and sharing their own "random" acts of kindness. If someone buys a coffee for the stranger behind them at a drive-thru and doesn't post about it, did it even happen?

JR: You keep an image of Gandhi, with the words, "Just finished day fifty of my hunger strike. #blessed," for just such an occasion.

WR: You'd rather see someone humblebrag about doing good than not see any good at all. Maybe their post will inspire others.

69. The Jackass is done with social media

. . . .

Hear ye, hear ye! Linda is leaving Facebook, and you all need to make arrangements accordingly! It will be easy to do—she's told you why she's leaving in great detail and listed many ways for you to reach her going forward. She's also replied to all the comments (a record number for her) with further details.

JR: You reply, "I thought you left a year ago," and throw a "Goodbye, Linda" party on Facebook Live.

WR: You update Linda's contact information and scroll on. Although you're a bit surprised, because Linda left your cocktail party early last week and didn't say goodbye to anyone.

70. The Jackass just woke up like this

. . . .

It's tough to pick the biggest lie on the internet. But somewhere after the Nigerian prince and "No, I wasn't ignoring you! Your email must have gone into my spam folder," we find the "I Just Woke Up Like This" Jackass. They're wearing makeup and have edited and filtered out every blemish, and they're backlit by three studio lights and lying in a perfectly designed bedroom they rented by the hour (yes, that's a real thing). Even the coffee cup has been selected for color and is spotlessly clean.

JR: You reply, "Back in my day, renting a room by the hour used to mean something else."

WR: You love the photos this Jackass shares; they're always so beautiful. You know they aren't exactly candid, but you don't care. Where can you get that gorgeous coffee mug?!

71. #thejackassuseshashtags

. . . .

#heyjackassifyouaregoingtouselonghashtagstocommunicate-
makesureeachwordbeginswithacapitaloryoumayenduplikethis

What's that? You're having trouble following along? Let's try this.

#HeyJackassIfYouAreGoingToUseLongHashtagsToCom-
municateMakeSureEachWordBeginsWithACapitalOrYouMay-
EndUpLikeThis

JR: You reply to each long, unreadable hashtag with your favorite of all time—#susanalbumparty (used by Susan Boyle and her promotions team to launch her album party)—and wait.

WR: Seriously, people, they're just hashtags. Get over it. #BiggerFishToFry

72. The Jackass is a hashtag hijacker

. . . .

These Jackasses use trending hashtags to promote themselves. They add a popular hashtag to their unrelated post and wait for the windfall.

JR: Put together a list of hashtags either no longer in the news (#Kony2012) or chronologically impossible (#Y2K, #Len-StealMySunshine) and reply with those.

WR: Some people actually use hashtags to itemize or time-stamp their thoughts, or for humor, so you understand that their reasons may not be sinister. #LetItGo

73. The Jackass was with you last night

. . . .

You wake up Sunday morning and check out Instagram, where you find you've been tagged in twenty-three photos from the bar last night. They aren't exactly the best photos, and you weren't really supposed to be out last night. This Jackass doesn't care—they tagged them all!

JR: You enthusiastically tag this Jackass in photos they aren't in. Extra points for photos of nights out they weren't invited to.

WR: You take your lumps for being out when you weren't supposed to and make sure to speak to that "friend" the next time you're together about tagging you without permission.

74. The Jackass works for the Oxford English Dictionary

. . . .

This Jackass was placed on Earth to make sure you use the right there, their or they're. As authors, we especially hate the grammar Jackasses. The best way to get comments about your new book or article is to make a spelling mistake or two! People love to correct, especially in public, and it sucks. You wouldn't believe how many people send us corrections after reading our book that's been printed, like we can magically make changes.

JR: You reply, "Thank you, their always some mistakes that slip through the cracks."

WR: You're just so happy they read the book! You make note of the mistake for future print runs and change it for digital versions.

75. The Jackass says Nazi, a lot

· · · · · · · · · · · · · · · ·

This Jackass throws the term "Nazi" around like a Frisbee. The barista who messed up their latte is a Nazi, the person who corrected their spelling or grammar is a Nazi, the teacher who sends home too much homework is a Nazi...

JR: This has to stop. For each offense, post the definition of Nazi as a reply.

WR: You message them privately and let them know some words can't just be thrown around.

76. The Jackass has really changed

. . . .

This Jackass took a great photo back in 2010 and they're holding it tight. We understand that was a good hair day and you were fifteen pounds lighter back then, but if your profile pic doesn't look anything like you, you're making a huge mistake.

JR: When this Jackass comes up to introduce themselves in real life, you hold up their profile pic for a side-by-side comparison and say, "Are you sure?"

WR: When meeting this Jackass, you keep your reaction to yourself. You get it; don't we all want to look our best in that tiny little photo? You went through a gazillion options before choosing yours and you're never going to change it.

77. The Jackass is humble

· · · · · · · · · · · · · · · · · ·

Let's consider a social media post like this (name changed to protect the guilty):

> Had the most incredible moment just now. Was heading down the escalator at the airport on the way to my sold-out event for 600 Fortune 100 CEOs in NYC and saw two business professionals headed in the opposite direction. One said: "Isn't that Captain Jackass from the 4,000-person business summit? He was the best keynote speaker I have ever seen in my life!" The other executive said, "OMG... his book changed my life and we bought it for every employee in the company and our stock went up 36% the following quarter." I'm humbled to help business leaders like this.

JR: You take the exact quote, change their name and put it in a book about Jackasses.

WR: You see right through this, of course—no one has ever spoken that way. But you also understand how hard it can be to promote yourself on social media without sounding like this guy, so you give them a like and go about your day.

THE JACKASS GOES TO SCHOOL

The Case of the Sister Scammer

· · · · · · · · · · · · · · · · · ·

If you listen to the *UnPodcast* or have read our bio in this book, then you know that between us, we have two university degrees. Both belonging to Alison. You also know that after some mergers and acquisitions we have five kids: one in grade school, three in high school, with one heading to university in the fall, and one a recent community college graduate. So, as you can imagine, we hear and share complaints about school. A lot.

A few years back, before our books and Scott's speaking career kept us busy, Scott was a human resources professor at our local college, and his alma mater, Sheridan College. Final project week was upon his Employment Law class, and he'd given out an essay assignment worth 35% of his students' final grade. One student emailed Scott asking for some feedback ahead of handing in the paper, and he was happy to help.

The student emailed him a five-page document, within which was a four-page essay. Scott read it and found it uncharacteristically good for this particular student (he hadn't exactly been a scholar all term). When he finished reading, he scrolled ahead to the fifth page, just to make sure he hadn't missed anything, and found a note from the student's sister. It read:

> This is the last time I'm writing an essay for you. I don't care what you tell Mom, I'm done with this.

When confronted, the student pretended unsuccessfully that the note was a joke. Scott let him know how lucky he was that he hadn't officially submitted the paper, or the consequences would have been very serious. Rather than hand him over to the school administration, Scott assigned him a new final project—a paper on ethics in the workplace—that he would be writing in class with Scott's supervision.

Too lazy to write his own paper, or even to proofread the one he plagiarized, the Sister Scammer is really the epitome of a school Jackass.

In school, we see all the same factors that lead to Jackassery as we do in the workplace—lots of people, pressure to perform, competition—plus we add in some hormones, up the balance of power and put a ton of pressure on kids to decide their future and achieve success. This is a time when we should be teaching our kids the Jackass prevention skills they'll need in the workplace. And so, in the following section, we provide the textbook for Jackass 101. Your teachers Mr. and Mrs. Stratten will be taking attendance. Please remove your hats and take your seats. Class is in session.

78. The Jackass doesn't have a question

· · · · · · · · · · · · · · · · · ·

This Jackass raises their hand in class, but never to ask a question. They just want to put in their two cents and make sure everyone knows they completed the reading and are a Smarty McSmarty Pants. They're convinced this class is all about them and take every opportunity to slow things down and talk about themselves. After graduating, this person continues this practice at meetings and during conference Q&As.

JR: You point toward them, and when they start to answer, you claim you were pointing at the student behind them. When they turn around to see who, you sprint out of the classroom.

WR: This Jackass sounds like a prime candidate for bonus assignments. You keep them engaged, allow others to participate and set a time limit on all "questions."

79. The Jackass thinks teachers are lazy

. . . .

This Jackass loves to say, "Teachers only work ten months a year." They've never taught a class, coached an early morning team sport or stayed up late marking papers.

JR: You hear this one a lot, so you have a reply loaded. "Until you have to wipe snot off the face of a kid that isn't yours, Jeff, how about you keep your thoughts to yourself."

WR: You take a deep breath and explain to this individual that teachers only get paid for ten months of the year, prorated over twelve months, and that this pay is woefully low compared with the value they bring.

80. The Jackass is a lazy teacher

· · · · · · · · · · · · · · · ·

In our son's high school history class, they are studying ancient Egypt, so the obvious choice when his teacher didn't have a lesson prepared (something that happens weekly, we're told) was to show the class the '90s "classic" *The Mummy*.

There are so many things wrong with this.

1 History is a content-rich subject. You have thousands of years of material to work with.

2 If you must take a day off a week, there are literally hundreds of hours of documentaries to choose from. There's an entire History Channel, for Pharaoh's sake...

3 If you have to pick something fictional, based in the historical era you're working through, there have got to be better choices than this rotten tomato. We'd rather they watched Indiana Jones. Brendan Fraser in *The Mummy* makes Brendan Fraser as Encino Man look educational.

The only other time we've seen Alison this angry at a teacher was when a Grade 10 English teacher told the same son that he didn't need to finish reading *To Kill a Mockingbird* because they'd be watching the movie in class. We fear for the future.

JR: You tell your child to skip class on movie days. May as well; they don't give detentions for skipping anymore. Plus, they really don't need to respect teachers, right?

WR: You wouldn't want to switch places with this underpaid, undervalued teacher. They once dreamed of using their bachelor's in history to travel the world unearthing treasures with a cool hat and whip, and now they spend their days surrounded by eye rolls from kids who barely put down their phones for class. They deserve that movie day more than anyone. Plus, it's likely the small break from work is what's keeping them from losing their goddamn, Brendan Fraser–loving mind.

81. The Jackass student *loves* group projects

. . . .

This Jackass just loves group projects, and then ends up being the one who contributes the least.

JR: You make the final page of the project a chart demonstrating group division of labor. Make sure to put "N/A" for Cody. If he calls you out on it, ask him to summarize your project's findings in two sentences or less. Hell, ask him what the title of the project is.

WR: You make it clear from the start that you will actually be tabulating everyone's effort. Seriously. Someone needs to put that person in check.

82. The Jackass teacher doesn't care about your other classes

. . . .

This Jackass is a professor who couldn't care less about your other courses. They must know that generally, students take more than one class at a time; they just don't care. This usually comes with a bad attitude and no consideration for the sprint across campus required to get to their class.

JR: You assume they've never worked in the real world, where time doesn't magically revolve around their schedule, so you set a timer to announce the end of lecture should they go even one minute over. We suggest using "TiK ToK" by Ke$ha.

WR: You do your best to follow their rules. It's one class, for only one semester, the results of which affect your future alone, not theirs. When you're a professor, you can be different.

83. The Jackass is out of office today

· · · · · · · · · · · · · · · · · ·

This Jackass has office hours, they just don't keep the office hours or have enough of them. We did a super informal, entirely unscientific survey of our Facebook friends and asked what some of their (or their kids') biggest pet peeves were about college, and this was number one. Not bad cafeteria food or overbooked classes. Not crowded or over-air-conditioned/heated or under-air-conditioned/heated dorm rooms. This professor gig would be so much easier if it weren't for all the students.

JR: You craft an "In/Out of the office" sign and keep it on your desk in class facing "Out." When the professor calls on you, just raise an eyebrow and point sarcastically at the sign.

WR: You understand the demands on a professor's time can be extensive, and keeping their door open a few times a week, plus email and other forms of communication, is plenty for you.

84. The Jackass only contributes in class to complain about bad wifi

. . . .

There have been days when our hazy-eyed teens only left their rooms willingly to ask why the wifi wasn't working. To this we say a hearty "get off our lawn!" Wifi is a miraculous invention that travels through space, magically providing us with directions and cute cat videos. Do you know how we had to get directions when we were in school? From an actual paper map! Or, worse, from an actual other human!

JR: Since you're the one with the PhD in this situation, you devote your research, time and energy to finding a way to block all wifi within a twenty-yard circumference of you at all times. On the first day of classes, you tell students your name is Dr. Nowifi and see how long it takes them to figure it out.

WR: Let's be honest here. When the wifi doesn't work, it's pretty irritating for everyone, including you. Plus, without the ability to contact you by email, your students would have to actually come and sit face to face with you ... perish the thought!

85. The Jackass needs a place to sit, stand and loiter, other people be damned

. . . .

Here we find our hallway talkers, sitters and slow walkers. Everywhere has the potential to be a resting spot for them! It's their world and we're just trying to get through it on our way to class.

JR: You organize a running of the teenage bulls through the halls of your school twice a day. That'll show them to sit on the stairs.

WR: You keep your eyes up and weave your way through the crowds in a manner that would make Michael Schumacher envious. Parkour may or may not be involved. Who needs the gym when every trip to class is a full-endurance escape room? If you stumble or fall, remember to get up, you son of a bitch, because Mickey loves ya.

86. The Jackass is a chatterbox

• • • • • • • • • • • • • • • • •

There's at least one of these Jackasses in each of your classes and project groups. Somehow, through years of kindergarten and *Sesame Street* and all the grades, they've managed never to learn to let other people speak. You seriously want to send them in for testing to see how they manage to get oxygen to their brains without seemingly ever having to take a breath.

JR: You enroll in an auctioneer class (which we assume exists), and the next time they pause for even a second, you enter into a tirade of epic proportions. This is what you trained for.

WR: You've never been much of a chatterbox yourself, so this Jackass is otherworldly to you. You listen, nod your head appropriately and thank your stars you won't have to do much talking with this one around.

87. The Jackass needs quiet

. . . .

This Jackass thinks they're your mom, or a librarian, and shushes you and everyone else every time you speak up. The thing is, the "Shhh" is louder than the original talking and rarely effective.

JR: All the shushing just makes you want to talk louder and more often. This Jackass isn't the teacher, and he certainly isn't lord and master over all audio in the school. You meet each shush with a spike in volume.

WR: You're just thankful you don't have to be the shusher! You've managed to outsource one of your least favorite things: having to tell people to be quiet.

88. The self-made Jackass

. . . .

They didn't go to college, and look how successful they turned out! Therefore, says this Jackass, kids don't need to go to college. And why stop there—just drop out of grade school! Oprah didn't graduate, so neither should you.

JR: You compile two lists: one of everyone you know who dropped out of school and is now penniless, and one of all the CEOs and billionaires who graduated. You keep these at the ready and send them out often.

WR: You aren't worried about your kids—they know where you stand. When you see this Jackass giving that advice to other people's kids, you share your positive education stories appropriately.

THE JACKASS IN TRANSIT

On the Jackass Road Again

· · · · · · · · · · · · · · · · · ·

We could write an entire library about travel and the Jackasses you meet (or become) along the way. Scott travels for a living, so he finds himself in planes, trains and rented automobiles more days than not.

Getting from A to B is a Jackass minefield. We're all just trying to get where we're going on time, without losing our cool. Scott, who is particularly affected by the Driving Jackass, has learned to control his anger by breaking out into song whenever he encounters frustration on the road. He does an impressive medley of "Why Aren't You Turning Right, It's Your Turn" and "Your Blinker Has Been On for Ten Miles" set to the tune of Europe's "The Final Countdown."

Air travel is particularly stressful, bringing together an expensive purchase, long lines, a ton of strangers, each with their own agenda, close quarters and being faced with our own mortality. It's basically a Jackass stew. So, after years of research with no arrests, here is our Air Travel Survival Guide.

1 Noise-canceling headphones. We can't say this enough: noise-canceling headphones are the best travel investment we've ever made. They protect against loud chewers, sniffers, crying babies, loud talkers, any talkers actually... and provide a steady, happy stream of movies, music, podcasts and audiobooks.

2 Never travel hungry or undercaffeinated. This protects against a variety of traveling Jackassery and sets you up to react to every Jackass with as little anger as possible. Let's be honest: we're all Jackasses when we're travel hangry.

3 Dress appropriately for travel. Airplanes are always too hot or too cold, and your seatmate turns their fan on and off 862 times per trip. Comfortable layers go a long way.

4 Organization. Know where your passport and boarding pass are, and have them ready. Put things that need to be removed for security within reach.

5 Take time to get the paperwork. Nexus, Clear, Global Entry and PreCheck have changed travel for us. We can't imagine how we ever traveled without them.

6 Alison's epitaph will read, "Here lies Alison Stratten. She only traveled with a carry-on." Invest in a carry-on suitcase that fits into overhead compartments and is easy to get from A to B. Our aversion to lines and waiting of any kind, and a few lost luggage experiences, mean that we only travel with carry-ons. Always. That means even if a trip includes multiple continents with a variety of weather, we make it work, and so can you.

7 Set a good example. Common courtesy (sadly, not so common) makes every trip go smoothly. Give up your seat to those who need it more than you, smile at the baby whose

mother boards the plane looking like she climbed Everest to get there, say please and thank you to airline workers and stay sober.

8   Be prepared, but not for anything. We have small pharmacies and charger stores in our luggage, but we don't pack everything. Most places we go have stores with items that might be needed in a pinch. No one needs three pairs of back-up shoes and ten outfits. A little planning and a little chill go a long way to packing like a pro.

Whether on the road, in the air or at a hotel, travel brings out the colicky baby in all of us. So take your seat, adjust your mirrors and for the love of tiny bags of peanuts, remember to pack your sense of humor. It's going to be a bumpy ride.

89. The Jackass weaves through traffic just to get a few cars ahead

· · · · · · · · · · · · · · · · ·

We get it: they're the most important person on the road. We assume wherever they're headed, it was worth nearly killing themselves, and others, weaving in and out of traffic only to end up beside us on the off ramp.

JR: Two can play at that game, Andretti. You rev your engine, glare over at them and press play on the *Fast and the Furious* soundtrack you downloaded for just such a situation.

WR: You make a note to book those extra driving lessons for the kids, then spend as much time beside Andretti at the light with your best "you know what you did" smile on.

90. The Jackass didn't have time to shave this morning

. . . .

This Jackass was too busy to eat this morning, or to shave, or to put on mascara, so they've transformed their car into a rolling Sephora/Starbucks. Obviously the manufacturer intended this use—look at all the mirrors in here!

JR: You decide to find out how well that makeup turns out when you slow down and let the Jackass rear-end you.

WR: This is why you wake up at 5:30—so you can get to work on time, fully dressed, made up and caffeinated.

91. The Jackass is on their phone

. . . .

Using your phone while driving is actually illegal around our parts, so this Jackass is really pushing their luck. All our luck, actually. They can be found at intersections, staring down into their crotch and smiling, or with their phones precariously mounted on the steering wheel.

JR: You guess since this Jackass is doing it, you may as well check Instagram too. This driving selfie is gonna go viral!

WR: Distracted driving is nothing new. Remember that lady who was putting on mascara at the light? You pat yourself on the back. Good thing some of us are paying attention.

92. The Jackass doesn't think the speed limit applies to them

. . . .

They drive slowly in the fast lane, speed through the slow lane, and generally change velocity at the drop of a hat. Clearly, those signs weren't meant for them!

JR: You were hoping for a drag race on the way to work today. Let's do this!

WR: They can weave around you all they want, you're doing the speed limit.

93. The Jackass is right behind you

This Jackass has watched too many Formula 1 races and is looking to save some gas drafting you all the way to work. They tailgate and are overly aggressive, and we bet they have metal balls hanging from their trailer hitch.

JR: You assume that guy back there wants you to slow down and teach him a lesson. This is why you pay for premium towing.

WR: If they wanna follow you all the way home, let them. At least you will know they're doing a reasonable speed. Besides, you put those bumper stickers back there for a reason.

94. The Jackass doesn't care about your vision

. . . .

High beams should be an add-on you earn once you've proven you're responsible enough to use them. This Jackass couldn't care less about oncoming traffic, as long as they can see the road. Probably because they don't realize other people exist.

JR: Two can play at that game! They probably weren't betting on you having the illegal, blind-everyone, light-up-the-darkness version of high beams. They really pay for themselves.

WR: Slow down and wait for them to pass you. You're not risking your safety any longer than absolutely necessary by driving near this Jackass.

95. The Jackass thinks this lane belongs to them

· · · · · · · · · · · · · · · · ·

This is the Jackass lane. It's all theirs, their precious. And they aren't letting anyone in, for any reason.

JR: You bide your time and stay close. Eventually this Jackass is going to need to change lanes, and you plan on being there to block them when they do. Totally worth driving an hour out of your way.

WR: Guess you'll ask the next person to let you in. Good thing not everyone is so possessive on the road.

96. The Jackass thinks this lane belongs to everyone else

. . . .

This Jackass may be a little too nice, because they're stopping traffic to let every single merging car into their lane as the rest of the cars wait behind them.

JR: That's it, you've had it. You're gonna swerve around this overly polite Polly and cut in front of her.

WR: This episode of the *UnPodcast* is amazing, and you've given yourself more than enough time to get to work. Let them *all* merge!

97. The Jackass will turn left, eventually

They have their signal on, so we assume this Jackass will eventually turn, maybe in two or three months. Until then, they just want you to know they're considering it.

JR: Jerry Seinfeld does a bit about drivers in Florida sitting low and driving slow. You know there's someone driving up there, you can see the top of their hat and their knuckles gripping the steering wheel with the strength of a gorilla. You're gonna honk until their hearing aids pick it up.

WR: You'll take slow, cautious drivers over maniacs any day. You can see from the whites of the knuckles that this guy means safety.

98. The Jackass needs that parking spot

. . . .

Being a Jackass does not qualify you for handicap and/or family parking. We don't care if you only had to run in for a second to grab quinoa. We don't care if you're in a rush and have to get home to feed your six cats. These spaces are not for you, and for a damn good reason. This is the same Jackass who takes more than one spot. Are you new? Because unless this is your first time parking a car or visiting a parking lot, you know what the lines mean.

JR: They've done it, so you might as well park in the "parent with young children" spot right beside them. After all, you did babysit your neighbor's cat once. That totally counts as child care.

WR: You snap a photo of their license and report them to the mall or grocery store or school, or wherever you are. They messed with the wrong neighborhood watcher!

99. The Jackass never gives up their seat

. . . .

This Jackass never gets out of their own head to look around them. Usually we support this kind of keep-it-to-yourself personality, but this is our exception. If someone could use that seat a little more than you, get up, buttercup.

JR: You walk over and sit in their lap. Clearly they've voided all rules of common decency, so you may as well teach them a lesson. Grab their hands and try to clip them together around you like a seat belt. After all, safety first.

WR: You give up your seat, offering it loudly enough for others to see and hear. "Good example" is your middle name.

100. The Jackass boards a plane

. . . .

Now boarding group Jackass! They stand up half an hour before boarding and crowd the entryway. They show no concern for others, for airport staff, or for the fact that they're actually boarding group C. Once on board, they commit every overhead-bin crime against humanity. They squish a giant bag into the overhead bin, which we assume they believe has a tiny Houdini inside it, ready to magically transform their duffle bag into a tote. Without concern for others, they flail madly, hitting fellow passengers with their bag, elbows and belly, as their shirt rides up.

JR: You take a photo of that bare, hairy midriff, tag it #PlaneMoron with your flight info and seat number and hope the internet finds him.

WR: You smile because you're sitting in first class. Can't swing a first-class seat? Your preparedness, excellent packing skills and latte make every seat feel luxurious.

101. The Jackass is in flight

. . . .

Once they're up in the air, why not walk around a bit and chat with their friends? This Jackass starts a bro country club in aisle 14, and they drink until they run out. No friends on the plane? That's OK, they'll just watch a couple movies without head-phones, so everyone can hear. We've sat beside a man watching *Taken* at full volume. This Jackass has a very particular set of skills. Skills he has acquired over a long career. Skills that make him a nightmare for people like you.

JR: You turn to the Jackass and tell him that Liam Neeson finds his daughter. He spoiled your flight, so you spoil his movie.

WR: You're so happy you invested in these noise-canceling headphones. Worth every penny.

102. The Jackass needs to pee

· · · · · · · · · · · · · · · · ·

Maybe if they have a weak bladder, they should have booked an aisle seat. Every time they stand up, they leave carnage in their wake—knocking over laptops and spilling coffee, often on your seat. Also, that curtain up there means the bathroom beyond it is for first-class passengers. Unless you have an unexpected emergency or are traveling with a young child, you can wait.

JR: When they come back from their fifth trip to the bathroom, you've moved all their stuff, half-spilled coffee and *Maxim* magazine to the center aisle.

WR: When they come back from their fifth trip to the bathroom, you've moved all their stuff, half-spilled coffee and *Maxim* magazine to your seat, and are sitting in theirs.

103. The Jackass needs fried chicken

. . . .

Airplane food may be crappy, but we're supposed to be in that crappiness together. Snacks are fine, even drinks, but this Jackass's bucket of extra crispy he bought in the terminal is way over the line.

JR: You tuck your napkin into your shirt and grab a piece of chicken from their bucket, eating it enthusiastically. Extra points if you offer some to the other passengers.

WR: You barely notice through the silence of your noise-canceling headphones and aroma of your coffee. You just love air travel!

104. The Jackass has pointy elbows

. . . .

Unless they have a nerve condition that has left them without feeling in their elbows, we're pretty sure they felt that jab too. One Jackass jabbed Scott with their elbow eleven times (yes, we counted) without a single apology.

JR: You've nicked the tiny plastic knife and have it ready to stab them back. Come on, do it. Make my day.

WR: Since the highest frequency of elbows occurs upon boarding and deplaning, you stay mindful and vigilant during these heightened times of attack. Tuck yourself away from the aisle as much as humanly possible and work on your business plan for travel suits of armor.

105. The Jackass has bare feet

. . . .

They've removed their shoes and socks and have their foot up on the armrest in front of them, so they may as well clip their toenails!

JR: You "accidentally" spill coffee on the foot of the person behind you. Problem solved.

WR: You travel with extra pairs of *Jackass Whisperer* socks and books to give away to the barefooted. You suggest to the stewards, pilots and gate agents that the airline make them official giveaways on every flight.

106. The Jackass doesn't share space

. . . .

Manspreaders and armrest hoggers, unite! They're like the liquid of people—they spread out to fill all available space, others be damned.

JR: You find bringing fried chicken on board and watching *Taken* without headphones really keeps your seatmate in their own space. Also, not wearing shoes and socks...

WR: You live and die by the shared seat rule and keep all limbs inside your quadrant where they belong. When you notice the spread, you nip it in the bud with a polite "excuse me" and place something right in the spot they were encroaching on.

107. The Jackass doesn't need a Kleenex

. . . .

They're a founding member of Sniffers without Kleenex (which, we have confirmed, is not an arm of Doctors without Borders). Clearly, their mom never taught them not to sniff.

JR: You shouldn't have to cover up your ears; you're not the rude one. Each time they sniff, you stand and, with a dramatic flip of the wrist, hand them a Kleenex. Maybe we should make *Jackass Whisperer*-branded tissues as well?

WR: Sniffing combined with the stress of air travel is basically Alison Kryptonite, and is the main reason she brings headphones, music and movies on every flight. Like a pro, you do the same.

108. The Jackass has arrived

. . . .

Thank the Flying Spaghetti Monster, the flight is over! This Jackass takes that seat belt off as soon as they hit the tarmac and stand up. They muscle ahead of everyone and pull their giant carry-on out of the overhead bin, elbowing and bumping along the way. Deplaning is about survival of the fittest, patience be damned!

JR: You stand up and do your best Roadblock from *G.I. Joe* impression, running into the prematurely standing passenger with the force of an offensive lineman on game day.

WR: You stay in your seat and let the stewards deal with this guy. Some people are just the worst.

109. The Jackass has a service squirrel

. . . .

According to the *Guardian*, police had to remove a woman from a flight because she boarded with an emotional support squirrel. This bright-eyed and bushy-tailed Jackass caused a two-hour delay. And really, ma'am, a squirrel? We guess all the emotional support badgers were taken. If you don't have a trained service animal that a doctor has supported you needing, stop it. You're why we can't have nice things.

JR: Three words: emotional support hawk. You find one, you train one, you reward them with squirrel meat and then you take one with you everywhere. Who's going to question someone with a hawk on their shoulder?

WR: You're just happy they were wearing shoes and socks. The Jackass, not the squirrel.

110. The Jackass hates your service animal

. . . .

While boarding, they loudly complain about the man ahead
of them and his support animal. After they're seated, they try
to pet the dog and sneak it some of their extra-crispy fried
chicken.

JR: You devote your evenings to researching ridiculous, fake
service animals and order a squirrel for your next flight.

WR: You aren't worried; the dog is better trained than the Jackass anyway.

111. The Jackass thinks children should be seen and not heard

· · · · · · · · · · · · · · · · ·

No one likes to travel beside a crying baby. Not even another crying baby. You're going somewhere important enough to defy gravity to do it. You've awoken, driven in traffic, dragged your belongings through security. There were lines and waiting and an unexplainable anxiety, even though you don't have any drugs, weapons or fresh fruits and vegetables. You've removed your shoes in public. All you want to do is watch a movie on a tiny screen and eat bad food off tiny cutlery, in peace. So when they find themselves sitting beside a crying baby and their apologetic parent, this Jackass just can't keep their angry eyes to themselves.

JR: You threaten a baby.

WR: You smile, pick up fallen toys and try your best to help out the worn-looking parent. We were all crying babies once.

112. The Jackass makes out in the elevator

. . . .

This Jackass treats hotel hallways, elevators and the check-in desk as their own personal space. Even with the plutonium-grade insulation we assume they think is in the walls, we can see and hear them fighting (or, shall we say, the opposite of fighting) with their significant other in any of these places.

JR: You do what Scott did recently. You open the hotel room door while standing in your robe and stare quietly at them until they notice you.

WR: You invest in some earplugs, and if it gets out of hand, you contact hotel security. They're used to it, and you don't need to get into an altercation in your bathrobe. Again.

113. The Jackass doesn't appreciate the hotel staff

. . . .

Front-line hotel staff are not second-class citizens, but you'd never know that from watching this Jackass. The hotel rate included a place to rest their head for the night; it did not guarantee they'd be waited on hand and foot, without gratitude, as they descend into the madness and mess of a frat boy.

JR: You take their toothbrush and . . .

WR: You understand that for some people, staying at a hotel is a bit of a vacation from reality and, therefore from cleaning up after themselves. This is why you have the Jackass's credit card on file.

THE JACKASS HAS A KID

1,000 Jackass Points to the Strattens!

. . . .

It was the first day of our sixth Disney Caribbean cruise. We'd gathered for the mandatory safety demonstration—picture the flight attendant safety dance, but with already inflated life jackets, a crowded deck filled with eager kids waiting to get their Mickey on and a lot of tired, overwhelmed-looking parents wondering if they should have saved the money for college/therapy. Once you've boarded the ship, this is the only thing everyone has to do. If everyone is on time and reasonably calm for attendance, the whole thing lasts about ten minutes. Of course, as you'd imagine, that ten minutes can feel like a lifetime to a hopped-up toddler with only this minutia between him and kid heaven.

We lined up with our kids, all teenagers with years of Disney experience under their belts. There was some minor pushing and shoving, and a lot of teasing about how Alison now had to line up at the front (damn you, height-based lineup). Beside us was a young rookie family with three children all under five years, two overwhelmed-looking parents, a stroller and their nanny.

We'll call them the Just-Barely-Keeping-It-Togethersons.

As they struggled to line up, the dad carried his eldest and pulled out every trick in the *Bribing a Kid Handbook.* We smiled understandingly and assured them it would be over soon and that there was child care and a spa on the horizon. This too shall pass.

Then, as our friendly Disney wrangler demonstrated the life vest, Mr. Just-Barely-Keeping-It-Togetherson dropped his son. Like, full on dropped him on the ground.

Tears and loud wailing began from the child. Mom grabbed him up, trying to quiet him, and we overheard Dad explain that the child had grabbed his sunglasses and stabbed him in the eye with their arm, and that's why Dad had dropped him on the ground.

Let the Jackassery begin.

Alison the Jackass made sure our kids knew that she'd traveled many times with three kids under five and never, ever dropped any of them, even without the help of a partner or nanny. And seriously, who needs a nanny on a cruise anyway?! The adults weren't even outnumbered! A one-to-one kid-to-adult ratio is like a vacation unto itself. Who can't keep a kid quiet for a few minutes?

The whole thing lasted about fifteen minutes. We smiled at the family and wished them good luck, then our kids ran off for food and we went to sit quietly with our books until dinner, feeling pretty damn good about ourselves and our choices. Maybe if other people didn't rely on a nanny all the time, their kids would be better behaved.

After dinner that evening, we went to a movie on the ship. And as Scott sat down with his 3D glasses in hand, he slipped and promptly stabbed himself in the eye with the glasses.

Call it Jackass karma.

He sat through the movie with one eye watering, tightly closed, in his best *Pirates of the Caribbean* impression. About ten minutes in, he leaned over, clearly in pain, and said, "I read this book about self-defense, and they tell you to go for your attacker's eyes first. Before his balls. We need to find that family and apologize. I totally would have dropped that kid. I would have dropped the most valuable Fabergé egg in the world. I would have dropped all our kids."

Being a parent is hard, like a plastic stick stabbing you in the eye repeatedly hard. Finding your parenting tribe (online and off) can provide you with a lot of support, but it can also leave you vulnerable to the world of parenting shame and blame that keeps us all feeling like we have no idea what the hell we're doing. So, let's take a dash of sleep deprivation, the guilt of a thousand sons (and daughters), and a whole lot of know-it-alls and leap into the world of the Jackass who has a kid. Protective eye gear not provided.

114. The Jackass wants to know when you're due

· · · · · · · · · · · · · · · · ·

This Jackass never learned not to assume someone is pregnant. They're related to the "Oh my god! You're HUGE, are you having twins??" Jackass and the "You must be ready to pop!" Jackass. We're going to save you a whole lot of pain, so listen very closely: unless she tells you to your face, or you can see the head, never, ever, ever assume a woman is pregnant.

JR: Your favorite reply is, "Yes I am, and the Big Mac I ate earlier is the father."

WR: You simply smile, pat your muffin top and let it go. After all, that means you're glowing, right?

115. The Jackass babysat once

. . . .

This Jackass once babysat their three-year-old neighbor while he napped and is convinced they're now a parenting expert. We've got some news for you: kids behave differently for their parents than for babysitters, especially when they're awake.

JR: Before you and your partner head out to that dinner and a movie, introduce your toddler to soda and Halloween candy. Stay away long enough for the experiment to be a wild success.

WR: Remember before you had kids? Take the unsolicited advice in stride and remember to add "may Jennifer have trip-lets" to your birthday wishes and evening prayers.

116. The Jackass knows it all

. . . .

This Jackass is the parent who knows everything. They've pro-created and kept said spawn alive this far, so obviously they know exactly what to do with your kids. You should be grateful for their presence.

JR: You engage in heated debates with them at every single opportunity. Your mom was right, you should have been a lawyer.

WR: They mean well, you know they do. If Carol gives her baby Jim Beam whiskey for teething and it works, good for them.

117. The Jackass loves a parenting debate

. . . .

Related to the know-it-all, this Jackass loves a good parenting debate. Their top two favorite topics are "stay at home versus work away from home" and "breastfeeding versus formula." They just can't get enough of the drama.

JR: You rage on, my parenting friend. You've done your research and are prepared with studies and data and personal anecdotes. Susan is never going to know what hit her!

WR: No mama drama for you. You simply respond with, "That's an interesting point of view," and go on being your awesome parenting self. You know the grass is always greener on the other side of the crib.

118. The Jackass is a pet parent

· · · · · · · · · · · · · · · · ·

This Jackass is convinced that they know everything about human parenting because they've got a dog/cat/gerbil. They want you to know their dog sleeps through the night, so your toddler should too.

JR: In the story introducing "The Jackass Online" section, we shared how Alison acted like a true Jackass about this one. You give angry eyes and loudly judge anyone who calls themself a pet parent, calls their pets their fur babies or uses a stroller or carrier with their pet.

WR: Don't be an Alison. Some people do love their dogs like children, and their choices don't affect you in anyway, so what's the harm? As Southerners would say, "Bless your heart."

119. The Jackass can't keep their mouth shut

· · · · · · · · · · · · · · · · ·

If we had a dollar for every time some random looked at our five kids and said, "Well, you sure have your hands full!" we wouldn't need to sell a single book. Our other favorites include: "You should let your hair grow so you look pretty, more like a girl," and "Why don't you make your son cut his hair? He'd be so handsome if he looked like a boy."

JR: You agree with whatever it is they said, totally ignore your kids or their reactions and remind them of the comment as often as possible.

WR: You value your kids so very much more than whoever this loud-mouthed stranger is, and you let them know it. If you think my hands are full, you should see my heart.

120. The Jackass is a social butterfly

. . . .

This one is for the kids. This Jackass parent seems to know everyone and stop every few minutes to talk to someone—mostly about their kids.

JR: You interrupt all social gatherings with a question like, "Mom, Dad called and said the feds are almost done at the house," or, "Mom, you finished the wine at breakfast. Want me to grab you another bottle?"

WR: You know it's better than your mom having no friends and spending every second with you. Because if you got all your mom's energy, you'd be a monster.

121. The Jackass wants you to know everything about their kids

. . . .

This Jackass shares personal stories about their kids online and off, never with permission. Not just the good stuff, but the failures and challenges too. It's not like their kids are ever going to grow up and read all that stuff they wrote about them. I'm sure the nursing home they choose will be top notch.

JR: Potty-training little Alexander is sending Jeff around the bend and he's been posting *all* about it. Lucky for you (and unlucky for Jeff), you've known Jeff for thirty years and have a plethora of embarrassing photos to share in the comments. "Remember when you pooped your pants in college, Jeff? Because I do and I have the photo to prove it!" *evil laugh*

WR: You set an example for your kids and leave Jeff and his posts alone. When your children grow up and read all the things you've written, they'll have a good example to follow— praise in public and criticize in private.

122. The Jackass can't live without peanuts

· · · · · · · · · · · · · · · · ·

This Jackass doesn't believe in allergies. They seriously take issue with having to skip the peanut butter sandwiches at school, at parties and at the Y. They don't care that someone else's child could get sick, or even die—they need their peanut butter cups. Right. Now.

JR: You teach your child to fake an anaphylactic episode and plan an elaborate revenge plot to teach this Jackass about consequences. Preferably somewhere public and on camera.

WR: This parent is not your friend nor worthy of your time. They don't believe in allergies? Allergies aren't Santa Claus. Well, you don't believe in having Jackasses for friends.

123. The Jackass needs help with the remote

· · · · · · · · · · · · · · · · · ·

This group of Jackasses has made you the official IT person for your family. It's a good thing you love them, or you'd change all their passwords to "penis."

JR: Might as well read all their emails and check out all their photos while you're on their phone. Maybe forward a few to yourself while you're here, and transfer yourself a nice payment from their online banking app.

WR: You decide to make it official. If you're IT around here, then everyone will be buying devices from your product line of choice, preferably one that comes with its own Geniuses.

124. The Jackass isn't IT

. . . .

You bought them their first computer and survived hundreds of hours hearing about *Minecraft*, but this Jackass couldn't care less. They may be your child, but they're not the IT department.

JR: If they aren't going to help you, then they aren't getting Nutella, or lasagna, or those burgers you make that take literally all day. If they don't feel like being your IT person, then you don't feel like being their parent.

WR: It's probably for the best—last time they sent themselves $500 from your banking app. Find tech support that doesn't come with teen angst and a dozen eye rolls.

125. The Jackass is registered at Saks Fifth Avenue

. . . .

This Jackass is having a party. They have lots of parties, actually. For each one, they expect lavish gifts and for you to invest in just the right outfit. There were engagement parties, bachelor parties, bachelorette parties, stag and does, rehearsal parties, weddings, post-wedding brunches, gender reveal parties... and having a baby hasn't slowed things down one bit.

JR: You make it your mission in life to either stop being invited or become known as the guest who always gives $10 iTunes cards and wears cargo shorts no matter the occasion.

WR: What better way to spend money than celebrating the joys of others! Go to the parties you can afford, and find excuses for the ones you can't.

JUDGEMENT- AND JACKASS-FREE MATH CLASS

. . . .

If you made it this far, there are a few things about you we know to be true (or untrue):

1 You think we're hilarious and are amazed at how we managed to sum up every irritating part of your day (in other words, you're a dirty liar who can't see your own Jackassery).
2 You're not offended. That's not the Whisperer way.
3 You are so incredibly offended you need to read the book multiple times cover to cover before crafting your all-caps angry Amazon review.

Basically, we know nothing. Thankfully, if you've been honest with your points, you should know something more about yourself. Turn to the inside back cover if you'd like some guidance on your level of Jackassery. Here's what we learned about ourselves:

Scott (Part-Timer and Freelancer) is a judgmental meat-atarian who's sorry you're offended he forgot to mention the spinach in your teeth. Relax. He's just telling it like it is. When you meet for lunch, between constant looks at his phone he flies into a rage if not given your undivided attention. When he looks up, he'll expect a medal for his presence and show you the video he made last week at the Imagine Dragons concert. It's mostly of the head of the dude in front of him, you were at the concert too and he already sent it to you (and a dozen other victims) in a reply-all avalanche last week, but you guess you'll just watch it again. Scott spends lunch complaining about how his mom is always asking for help with her iPad and the injustice of "12 items or less" lines at the grocery store. Clearly, he can't be trusted. He tagged you in that Imagine Dragons post on Facebook even though you told him you were supposed to be finishing up a group project that night. Scott's in the group, too, but he doesn't care because someone (you) always get his work done for him. He offers you a ride home after lunch, but there's no way you're getting in his car again! Last time he wove in and out of traffic, impossibly both letting no one into his lane and letting everyone in, probably because he was on his phone the whole time. So you let him know you have your own car and leave as he goes around the restaurant talking to everyone like the social butterfly he is. It's hard to imagine you once made out with him in a Hilton elevator...

Alison (Associate) is an equally judgmental vegetarian who's slightly less sorry you were offended about the spinach she failed to mention in your teeth. She once told you to wear a different shirt in a presentation ... after the presentation was over. When you meet her at the mall, she's always either on her phone or one-upping your story about skydiving with chinchillas. She just can't believe you haven't tried troga or read Michelle Obama's book! Seriously, what's the matter with you? At the mall, she's a situationally deaf nightmare. You tried to get out of this get-together, but when you weren't quick enough to reply to her email, she went deep on Google and found your old high school wrestling team photos and threatened to send them to everyone. As you walk around, she never shuts up, telling stories about her last flight to New York, where her Jackass seatmate put her magazine and coffee in the aisle during her sixteenth trip to the first-class bathroom. After the mall, you head over to the gym, where Alison seems completely unaware of just how sweaty she leaves her equipment. At least she didn't cancel on you last minute again, and this time she only posted five pictures of her workout, so that's something. While you sweat, she loudly offers up parenting advice and complains about her kids never helping her with the remote. It's hard to imagine you once made out with her in a Hilton elevator...

So here, dear readers, is the big question: Is this who Scott and Alison are?

First, Alison has clearly skewed her results by leaving out the mall points and because she's never worked in an office. We all know she's an even bigger Jackass. Second, because the authors chose the Jackasses to look at, their results will be biased toward things that irritate Scott and Alison. You may have a whole 125 other Jackasses that bug you. That's the thing with Jackasses—they're in the eye of the beholder.

Sure, that one time Janice swiped through all your photos, but she also drove you to the airport last week. She's not all bad. None of us are. Not even Alison. That said, if we are always running into Jackasses wherever we go, then maybe the common denominator is us. We're all the Jackass and we're also all the Whisperer, and sometimes the difference between the two is a cup of coffee and a well-timed gate arrival before a flight. It's that easy. Say kind things to others, be considerate of their time and share space more often than you share your own opinion.

Add up your score and see how you did. Anything surprise you? We'd love to hear all about it. You can reach us on Twitter at @UnMarketing and @UnAlison, or on the UnMarketing Facebook page. Photo evidence? Instagram works too! Reach us at @UnMarketing and @AlisonRobin there. You can also visit www.JackassWhisperer.com, where you can add any Jackasses we've missed to the Jackass database or email us at Donkey@JackassWhisperer.com. You can listen to Scott and Alison on the *UnPodcast*, on iTunes or wherever you get your podcasts. And last, if you're looking for the best keynote speaker in the universe, check out Scott at www.UnMarketing.com.

AUTHORS' NOTE (OF APOLOGIES)

. . . .

Scott and Alison would like to formally apologize to the following:

Anyone named Carol, Linda, Jeff, Arugula, Janice, Joe, Swol, Christinith, Kevin, Cody, Chad, Jennifer, Susan, Steven or Donald or married to someone named Donald

Fans of John Wick, Mario Andretti, the Backstreet Boys, Bob Dylan, RuPaul, Ke$ha, Michael Schumacher, Bell Biv DeVoe, *Game of Thrones*, Arugula, Skrillex, R.E.M., Emily Post, Metallica, Susan Boyle, *Xanadu*, MacGyver, Dustin Hoffman, Brad Pitt, Beyoncé, Gandhi or the beautiful city of Des Moines

Scott's sister

Chinchillas

People actually raised in barns

People who like banana, mayo and cilantro sandwiches

Alison's high school boyfriend

Pet parents

Nigerian princes

Our moms, for complaining about helping you fix your iPads

Brendan Fraser and anyone involved with the making of *The Mummy*

Anyone who didn't already know the ending of *Taken*

Anyone with an emotional support squirrel

People who hang metal balls from their trailer hitches

Our children

We're terribly sorry you were offended,

Scott Stratten

and

Alison Stratten

ABOUT THE AUTHORS

. . . .

Scott and Alison Stratten are Jackass experts, co-authors of five bestselling business books, co-owners of UnMarketing Inc. and co-hosts of not only the *UnPodcast* but also five children, three dogs and one cat. Their books, their company and their show all represent their thoughts on the changing world of business through their experiences of entrepreneurship, two degrees (Alison), not lasting long as an employee (both) and screaming at audiences around the world (Scott; Alison is more polite). They were put on this earth as a reminder that not all Canadians are passive and apologetic. Businesses like PepsiCo, Saks Fifth Avenue, IBM, Cirque du Soleil and Microsoft have been brave enough to want their advice. They now spend their time keynoting around the world, and realizing they rank tenth and eleventh in order of importance in their home.

www.UnMarketing.com
www.JackassWhisperer.com
#JackassWhisperer